Proverbs for Parenting

There Is a Manual

KRISTIN OVERMAN

ISBN 978-1-63784-435-9 (paperback)
ISBN 978-1-63784-436-6 (digital)

Copyright © 2024 by Kristin Overman

All rights reserved. No part of this publication may be reproduced, distributed, or transmitted in any form or by any means, including photocopying, recording, or other electronic or mechanical methods without the prior written permission of the publisher. For permission requests, solicit the publisher via the address below.

Hawes & Jenkins Publishing
16427 N Scottsdale Road Suite 410
Scottsdale, AZ 85254
www.hawesjenkins.com

Printed in the United States of America

CONTENTS

Preface: Parenting: There Is a Manual..v
Introduction: A Job That Requires a Manual............................vii
Chapter 1:   Introduction to Proverbs 1

Section 1:   Establishing a Foundation for God's
               Way The Simple—Instruction Stage

Chapter 2:   The Fear of the Lord—Don't Obey Me....................13
Chapter 3:   The Fear of the Lord (Part 2)—Reproof...................24
Chapter 4:   Listen, My Son (Part 1)—Children 35
Chapter 5:   Listen, My Son (Part 2)—Parents 47
Chapter 6:   Beware 52
Chapter 7:   Wisdom 58
Chapter 8:   A Transcendent Pattern 66
Chapter 9:   Wisdom: The Person and the Relationship 72

Section 2:   Growing Independence—Building
               Character in the Youth—The Conversation Stage

Chapter 10:   A Comparison of Two Ways 83
Chapter 11:   The Sovereignty of God—A Second Appeal to God 99
Chapter 12:   Anger—Avoid, Slow, Stop, and Control 106
Chapter 13:   Words and the Tongue 113

Section 3:   Complete Independence—Skill
               with Responsibilities—The Adviser Stage

Chapter 14:   Wine and Drunkenness 123

Chapter 15: Workers—The Skill of Managing and
 Leading People 130
Chapter 16: Wealth—The Skill of Managing Money and
 Materials 137
Chapter 17: A Warrior Woman—Do Not Give Your
 Strength Away 144
Chapter 18: Conclusion—What Does the Manual Tell
 Me to Do? 152

PREFACE

Parenting: There Is a Manual

After I gave birth to my first son, I was talking to a friend who had a son of her own. She kindly shared some of her experiences as a parent. She had been a mom a little longer than I had, so I listened intently. She told me that the Bible gives little instruction on how to raise kids. Besides a few verses in the New Testament about children obeying their parents, her belief was that the Bible was silent on parenting. I hadn't been a parent long, but if there was anything I knew about God, it was that He gave us what we needed for every task that He called us to. I was heartbroken at her perspective. He would not give us the blessing of children and omit instructions on what to do with them. People joke all the time that there is no manual on parenting, but this is untrue! Second Peter 1:3 says that God has given us everything for life and godliness. That includes parenting. Yes, the Bible doesn't spell out how many feedings you should do at three months or how to potty train a child with sensory issues or what age your teenager should start dating, but it is far from silent on parenting.

When I was a teenager, my youth pastor encouraged me to read Proverbs every day from the time I was sixteen to twenty-five. I followed his advice. Yes, I missed days, but Proverbs was consistently part of my time with God. The sayings and truths in it would constantly pop up in my mind. Almost ten years of daily reading will do that to you. When my first three children were young, I took two years to study Proverbs on my own. I literally tore the book apart. The treasures the Holy Spirit revealed were more precious than gold, just as Proverbs says. I found that God's plan for life is the best.

I admit that, at times, I don't know what to do with my kids. God has paired sinful parents and sinful children in His perfect plan. However, God doesn't want us to stay in our sinful or naive ways, nor should we allow our children to do so. God, in His Word and through His Spirit, will help us when we do not know what to do. God has created parents to be the first teachers and influencers of their own children. Through tears, prayers, and the search for wisdom, God has met me every time I did not know what to do. I have been stuck and at a loss, but I don't stay there because I know the perfect Parent who knows all the answers. His Word has wisdom, and His Spirit leads us to it. I believe 2 Peter 1:3 that He has given me everything for life and godliness, including parenting! Proverbs is my favorite book in the Bible. It is a manual for parenting but also for a life lived in God's way. I hope that you enjoy it as much as I have!

INTRODUCTION

A Job That Requires a Manual

Parenting is a job. It is a responsibility that is hard work. You will sleep less and be frustrated, tired, and scared. Being a parent is the most important job in the world, and yet so many of us are the least prepared for it. We study for college to pursue a career. We train for a job. We read textbooks and practice through internships. We observe coworkers or a mentor to improve our trade. We take continuing education classes or go to conferences to increase our knowledge. At the end of our lives, the jobs we did will matter, but will they matter as much as the people standing at our bedside?

When my grandpa died, he was surrounded by his wife, four children, and three daughters-in-law. At the end of life, the things that matter most are the people we impact, and the people we are to impact the most are our children. Our children carry on our habits, our ideas, our beliefs, and our convictions. Don't we want to pass on the best ideas and the best habits to our kids? We need to get these from God's Word, and Proverbs is one of the key books for it.

For this to happen, two things are required of parents. First, they must be wise themselves. They must know the wise Proverbs in order to pass them on. They must understand them well enough to recognize them in daily circumstances in order to point them out to their children.

Second, parents need to spend time with their kids. Deuteronomy 6:7 says we are to teach our children diligently when we sit, walk, rise up, and lie down. We cannot instruct them diligently if we are too busy to spend time with them. You cannot influence someone you don't interact with. Instructing and teaching require time.

Job methodology—the four verbs of God's Word and way

Let's go to the New Testament for a second and look at what it says about using God's Word. Second Timothy 3:16 says, "All Scripture is inspired by God and profitable for *teaching*, for *reproof*, for *correction*, for *training* in righteousness." These four verbs tell us how to keep on God's path. *Teaching* is imparting knowledge about the right way. *Reproof* is when we warn of the wrong way. *Correction* brings them back to the right way when they have left the correct path. *Training* in righteousness helps keep them on the right way. Training is the discipline, the actual practice. We'll see this in Proverbs also. Concepts are repeated over and over. Proverbs gives us the content. These four verbs are the method. Parenting is constantly teaching, reproving, correcting, and training our kids to stay on God's path.

In this book, we will use Proverbs to do the following:

- teach—show the right way
- reprove—warn of the wrong way
- correct—bring back to the right way
- train—practice to keep on the right way

But my kid is different!—truths that are constant

Ecclesiastes says that there is nothing new under the sun. This includes kids. You may have a child with a disability, a disease, or an absent father. Whatever the situation, God says there is nothing new under the sun. Man has dealt with the same problems throughout history. God's principles and truths apply to us as they did to people hundreds of years ago. We may have to adjust them or repeat them more with certain kids. If we believe 2 Peter 1:3 and 2 Timothy 3:16, we can believe that God's plan in Proverbs will work for every kid. If we desire to live in the abundance and victory that God has given us, we need to believe that He has given us everything we need for life and godliness, including our unique child. If we think we know it all, we are being prideful. If we are not willing to change, we are not being teachable. If we do not think it will work, we are not believing God's Word. If we are not willing to find a solution, we are being lazy. We must start with trust in God and His ways.

I am a strong-willed person. I have a quiet stubbornness. I relate to Jacob, who wrestled with God. He would not let go of God until God blessed him. When I ask for wisdom and help, I trust that God will give it. Every single time I have struggled with something with one of my children, God has always been faithful and met my need for help. I had to ask and pray. I searched for answers in His Word, in other biblical books, and in the wisdom of others. It may have taken time, but He was always faithful.

There are two prayers in Scripture that God says He will always answer yes to. One of them is the prayer for wisdom. James 1:5 says, "But if any of you lacks wisdom, let him ask of God, who gives to all generously and without reproach, and it will be given to him." The second is the Holy Spirit. In Luke 11:11 and 13, Jesus said, "Now suppose one of you fathers is asked by his son for a fish; he will not give him a snake instead of a fish, will he? If you then, being evil, know how to give good gifts to your children, how much more will your heavenly Father give the Holy Spirit to those who ask Him?" God guarantees that He will give us wisdom and His Holy Spirit if we ask. We need to ask for those as parents.

Principle versus application

Before we start, I want to define some terms concerning Bible study. There is a difference between a principle and a practical application or experience. When I have talked to people struggling with parenting situations, they want a three-step program. "Just tell me what to do. Give me a system with steps that work." Our approach should instead be, "What am I not understanding? What do I need to learn?" The problems and issues we deal with are more about what we, as parents, believe. Our beliefs come out in our interactions with our children. If you take away anything from this book, let it be that *parenting God's way starts with thinking God's way*. Parenting God's way means understanding His methods and ideas before using them.

The Bible is full of principles and concepts for parenting. The principles are the constant truths we need to know from Scripture. Not every principle is applied the same way to everyone. We need to draw the principle from Scripture and then have the wisdom to use the principle with each child. The practical application of what I do may not work for you because God did not make me like you, nor did He make my children like yours. In this book, I will go through and explain to you the principles in Proverbs and give you examples of how I use the principle. But my examples may not work for your child. I said before that the Bible doesn't tell us exactly how to feed babies, potty train toddlers, or date. But it does tell us the principles behind those. It teaches us how to use discernment and wisdom even with an infant. It shows how to train a young child, whether it is about kindness or the potty. It gives us ideas about marriage and sexual relationships that we can pass on to our teens. God has allowed for creativity in the application because He made us creatively. If the Bible were "easy" to apply, it would be a comprehensive list of dos and don'ts. But God wants us to use our thinking for the concepts and our creativity for the application.

Each chapter in this book will go over the principle or truth taught in Proverbs. I give you examples of how I use it and then a challenge for you to pray and ask God how to use the principles in your home with your children. That is what wisdom is: understanding the principle so well that you can apply it in different situations and with different children.

I pray that through this book, I can help you understand the principles. As you better understand them, my prayer is that you will gain wisdom and have the creativity to apply them in your family, environment, and time. Rely on the Holy Spirit to help you. He guides and counsels.

Whether you are about to be a parent or you already have children, it is never too late to refine your skills and look at God's way of doing life because He has given you a manual for this job! Let's look at it.

Practical Proverbs for the family

These are some self-reflective and discussion questions for parents as you get started.

Questions for parents:

- Do you consider parenting a job that requires a manual? Do you need instructions on how to do this job?
- What two things do you need to impart the wisdom of Proverbs to your children?
- How can you better know the truths in Proverbs?
- Look up 2 Timothy 3:16. What are the four verbs that Scripture is good for? Can you explain these?
- Look up Luke 11:11–13 and James 1:5. What are the two things God always will answer yes to? Do you believe this?
- Do you believe 2 Peter 1:3 that He has given you everything for life and godliness? If you have made excuses for your child's behavior or have areas where you have no idea what to do, write them down. Ask God to give you what you need.
- Can you explain the difference between principles and application? Can you give an example of each?

CHAPTER 1

Introduction to Proverbs

The manual's purpose and table of contents

Principle: Proverbs lists three types of people in three sections. Solomon reintroduces himself in each section for three levels of instruction: a foundation in God's way, conversations of God's way, and advice for God's way.

Sayings

When I first started studying Proverbs, I was frustrated. I told you earlier that I tore the book apart. Well, the book seemed sporadic. Solomon randomly listed sayings that didn't seem to fit together. He would talk about anger in one verse and money in the next. I could not understand why he had not made comprehensive sections—one on wisdom, one on women, one on work, anger, and so forth. Then we could access all the information on wisdom in one area, look up the information on anger in another, etc. Why so many short sayings? Why couldn't he explain everything about one topic all at once? As I wrestled with the text, I saw that there was an organization, and there was a purpose for the organization.

The Holy Spirit brought to mind Deuteronomy 6:4–7: "Hear, O Israel! The Lord is our God, the Lord is one! You shall love the Lord your God with all your heart and with all your soul and with all your might. These words, which I am commanding you today, shall be on your heart. You shall teach them diligently to your sons and shall talk of them when you sit in your house and when you walk by the way and when you lie down and when you rise up." Proverbs was not meant to be long lectures. It was supposed to be an example of the tiny bits of wisdom we pass on to our kids as we talk of life—sitting in our house, walking by the way, lying down, and rising up. Proverbs is Solomon living out Deuteronomy 6. It was Solomon walking around his palace with his son, observing nature and people, and talking about wisdom. As the Israelites worked, cooked, talked, went to bed, and got up in the morning, they were to instruct their children about God. Proverbs was a compilation of small truths given in the normal routines of the day. It is a compilation of wise sayings that parents can use to teach their children as life happens.

Proverbs are short little sayings to explain something, to teach a lesson, to give an example, and to pass on wisdom. Proverbs comes from the Hebrew word *Mashal,* which means "to be like, to represent something, or to compare." Many ancient cultures had proverbs. The Egyptians did. Confucius in China did. Later philosophers like Socrates used proverbs to discuss and teach. Remember, most people at this time were illiterate. Information was passed down orally. Because nature was something common to everyone, it was used to exemplify concepts and inanimate truths.

The theme—wisdom

The main theme of Proverbs is wisdom, the ability to acquire knowledge and to apply it skillfully to life's situations. My youth pastor defined wisdom as a "skill in godly living." Have you ever seen someone skilled in life? They can handle relationships. They get along with people or can deal with conflict well. They succeed and enjoy their work. They have the discipline to save money, work out, and eat well. People enjoy their company. They are good at life. They suffer well when hard times come. They don't follow the crowd and trends. They know what they believe and stand in that confidence. Do you realize that is what God wants for us? That is the abundant and wise life. It doesn't mean things are perfect and without struggle. Proverbs is about how to live life in God's way.

Purpose

In chapter 1, Solomon gives us a list of seven purposes for the book and the three people he wrote for:

- to know wisdom and instruction
- to discern the sayings of understanding
- to receive instruction in wise behavior, righteousness, justice, and equity
- to give prudence to the *naive*
- to give *youths* knowledge and discretion
- to help the *wise* to hear and increase learning
- to understand a proverb, a figure, the words of the wise, and their riddles.

Here, Solomon is giving his purpose and goal. It is as if he says, "By the time I am done raising you this is what I want you to have and be able to do, son. I want you to know what wisdom is and what instruction is. These two first things are going to be the key to life. Instruction is the means, so you better pay attention. Second, I want you to be able to discern the sayings of understanding. Discernment is the ability to make decisions. You, son, need to have the ability to make wise choices. Third, I want you to receive instructions in these four different areas of life: wise behavior or conduct, righteousness or doing right because it is right, justice or acting according to godly law, and equity or fair treatment."

Solomon wants his son to be good at life. A wise person will know right and wrong, be able to make wise decisions, do right things, act justly, and be teachable.

Then he lays out a growing process: the naive, the youth, the wise. When you are young and naive, you need to have prudence, cautiousness, and common sense. You need to think about things before you do them. As you gain prudence, you need to grow in knowledge and discretion. After you have developed this skill of stopping and thinking, you need to have more knowledge to draw from in order to make wise decisions. When you are wise, I want you to increase in learning and understand the words of those wiser than you so you become more so.

Solomon sets goals for his son. Not physical or personal aspirations but his goals as a parent. It is as if he asks himself, "What do I want my kid to leave with?"

When my kids were little, I listed the skills and knowledge I wanted them to leave my home with. Following is a journal entry from December 17, 2010:

My goals for my children:

- know God, love God, obey God
- have the ability and skills to get along and deal with people
- grow to be an adult who is self-sufficient, well-mannered, hardworking, and balanced in the different areas of life
- have godly habits and set goals
- be purposeful
- rely on God in every circumstance
- have a godly perspective, not a worldly one

Since then, I have refined it to three things. I want my kids to know godly ideas, have godly habits, and set godly goals by knowing, loving, and obeying God. All the practical things fall into three areas God has given us to manage: our resources, our responsibilities, and our relationships.

Having an end goal helps us know what we are doing with our kids. Parenting is more than planning birthday parties and driving children to sporting events. Parenting is imparting God's truths and ways to a future generation. The Bible talks about this in Psalm 78:4: "We will not conceal them from their children, but tell to the generations to come the praises of the Lord, and His strength and His wondrous works that He has done." The job of parenting, in God's eyes, is to teach His ways and His truths. The greatest disciples you will make are your children. Determine at the beginning what you want the end to look like.

The manual's table of contents

Proverbs is laid out like a manual. So yes, you can go to a section and get help for little ones, growing kids, and teens! I'll show you how. I said before that Solomon mentioned a growing process in his table of contents. There are three types of people he lists: the naive, the youth, and the wise. These three types of people are seen throughout Proverbs. There are different characteristics at each level, different content and skills to teach at each level, and a different focus. Let's first look at these.

The three people

Naive literally means simple. The naive is the young child. The young child defines everything simply. They know little of life. They are self-focused, getting upset when they don't get what they want. The naive are not aware of the danger. Parents need to teach them caution and common sense. Young children cannot understand other people's feelings or perspectives. When I taught kindergarten, my students would do show and tell. I always had some students who would hold their show-and-tell items facing themselves instead of toward the other children. They could not grasp the idea that they could see their item, but others could not because they could not see another's viewpoint. The naive need the simple facts: "This is dangerous," "This is wrong," "Listen to this person," and so on. The naive need to listen, learn, and obey.

Youths need knowledge and instruction. They need to understand how life works, what things are for, how they can steward relationships and basic ideas of responsibility. They are working out how to do life. They will observe and wonder: If God is good, why do bad things happen? How do you do laundry? How do you deal with conflict or emotions? How do you earn money? The youth need conversation to understand.

Finally, *the wise* are going to increase in learning. They are still refining their skills and increasing their knowledge. They want to improve, so they receive feedback. They are evaluating relationships, making the right choices, and deciding between good and best. This stage is when we are preparing our kids to leave. As parents, we become advisers as our children are carefully trying out the foundation that has been laid. This stage doesn't end. The wise continue to increase in learning their whole life. If we have been wise, we have established a love of learning and a love of God, so the pursuit of wisdom never ends. The wise need chances to apply wisdom and specialized wiser ones to learn from.

Proverbs can be divided into three sections based on the three types of people or stages. You can easily identify the three sections because, at the beginning of each, Solomon reintroduces himself. It is like Solomon is aware of each new phase of his son's life and begins it with a new conversation: "Hey, son, I'm going to give you some instruction and advice for this stage of life. You will face some new things, and here is some new knowledge and skills."

The three sections

Proverbs 1 through 9 lay a foundation of instruction. It includes the fear of the Lord, listening, obeying authority, being aware of sinners, and recognizing wisdom. Remember, the naive do not have enough common sense to keep themselves safe. They need an understanding of authority, training in proper response to authority, the skill of listening, being aware of sinners, and recognizing wisdom. In this first section, Solomon addresses the recipient as "my son."

The second section is for the youth. It includes wisdom about character, hard work, honesty, anger, friendship, and self-control. In this section, Solomon steps back a little and does not refer directly to his son. He talks conceptually about *the man* or *a man*.

Solomon helps his son understand and go beyond facts by comparing and giving examples. He is encouraging his son to think like a wise person by evaluating behaviors and choices. He is teaching the son to practice discretion by evaluating and making the decisions himself. Solomon gives a lot of examples and images so the son can see the concept in various circumstances. These chapters compile the biggest section from chapters 10 to 24: the conversation and explanation stage.

The last section is for the wise. Topics include money, work, women, leadership, addictions, and drunkenness. In chapters 25–31, the parent steps back and gives more advice than instruction. The recipient is called *the king* or *a ruler* (a position of authority and responsibility). The son is getting ready for a position of responsibility or is already in it. Several of these chapters were not authored by Solomon. They were written or said by moms. It is like momma's last words before she lets her son go. Notice this last section is smaller—only seven chapters. This is the advice stage.

I've divided this book into those three sections. I have organized the topics within each section so we can look at each topic comprehensively.

Section 1 Foundation	Section 2 Conversation	Section 3 Advice
Proverbs 1:1 The Proverbs of Solomon, son of David, king of Israel.	**Proverbs 10:1** The Proverbs of Solomon. A wise son makes a father glad, but a foolish is grief.	**Proverbs 25:1** These also are the Proverbs of Solomon—the heart of kings.
Introduction and Foundational teachings Proverbs 1–9	Chapters 10–24	2 Oracles chapters 25–31
To the naive—young, simple ones My son	To the youth The man of…	To the wise A king
Topics: Fear of the Lord Listen Beware sinner's enticement Wisdom	**Topics:** Wise character Comparisons of two ways of life God's way versus man's way Anger Tongue Work Relationships Responsibility	**Topics:** Wise stewardship Wealth Work Wine Addiction Wife Leadership

Literary form—a tool for us to teach too!

To understand Proverbs well, it is important to understand how it is written. Proverbs is Hebrew poetry. Its function was more than just beautiful language. It was also for learning and memorization, a teaching tool. I'll show you throughout the book how you can use the way it was written to help your children learn and understand it. There are embedded tools for parents to use.

Proverbs uses great imagery to explain concepts such as wisdom, foolishness, anger, discretion, understanding, and more. Proverbs attaches inanimate concepts to animate images, such as parts of the body, architecture, and nature.

Proverbs also utilizes literary elements that we do not have in English. One of them you will see often is parallelism, an idea that is repeated either by restating it or contrasting it. Another literary device we will see is personification, an inanimate or conceptual idea explained with human attributes. Proverbs personifies wisdom and foolishness. What a great way to explain these two concepts by bringing them to life!

A quick note about the author

Solomon is the main author of Proverbs. He lived in 900–950 BC. Solomon was the third monarch of Israel after Saul and his father, David. He was rich, lived in a palace, and was well-educated. Solomon lived in peacetime. He did not have to fight wars like his father, David, had. He had time to be more intellectual and reflective. He built the first temple for God, one of the wonders of the ancient world. He is described by the Bible as the wisest man. God told Solomon to ask Him for anything He wanted, and Solomon asked for wisdom (1 Kings 3–4). His wisdom was known throughout the world.

First, Kings 10 records the visit of the Queen of Sheba and describes Solomon's wisdom. The queen tested him with difficult questions, and he answered all of them. Solomon's wisdom was displayed in the house he had designed and built, the food at his table, his diet, and the seating or ranking of his servants. His wisdom was displayed in the attendance of his waiters, cupbearers, and their attire.

The Queen of Sheba states in verse 8 that his men and servants were blessed to stand before him and hear his wisdom. Solomon carried out justice and righteousness. He was God's tool to reveal this great book.

Concluding prayer

> Dear Lord,
>
> Thank You for Your word. Thank You for communicating to us Your plans, desires, and ways. As we look at Proverbs, may Your Holy Spirit teach us and convict us. Help us to use what we learn in our lives and with our families. May Your word transform our minds so we may please You. In Jesus's name, amen.
>
> Verse to pray: Psalm 139:23–24

Practical Proverbs for the family

As you go through the exercises at the end of each chapter, always start with the naive section. Build the foundation and then go up.

The naive
- Read in a picture Bible the stories about Solomon.
- Introduce him as the author of Proverbs. Who was he? What did he do for God?

The youths
- Read the following Scriptures and list what you learned about Solomon's wisdom. In what areas of life did he have wisdom? How did he have it? Why did he have it? How is it displayed?

    o In 1 Kings 3:1–15, Solomon asks for wisdom. List why he asks.

- 1 Kings 3:16–28
 - 1 Kings 4
 - 1 Kings 10:1–9

The wise
- Read Ecclesiastes
- Solomon was wise, but he did not end life well. He had everything—wealth, women, power, fame, pleasure. What does he say about life in Ecclesiastes 12:13? What matters in the end? Compare this to Proverbs 1:7.

Parent reflection and application

- Write down your parenting goals. What do you want your children to know when they leave home?

SECTION 1

Establishing a Foundation for God's Way
The Simple—Instruction Stage

The first section of Proverbs is written to the naive. Proverbs chapters one through nine give this foundation: the fear of the Lord, listening, warnings, and wisdom.

The foundations are the following:

1. Fear of the Lord
2. Heeding the instruction of your father
3. Not consenting to sinners who entice you
4. Recognizing and following wisdom

CHAPTER 2

The Fear of the Lord— Don't Obey Me

*The Fear of the Lord is the beginning of knowledge.
Fools hate wisdom and instruction.*

—Proverbs 1:7

Principle: Establish God as the ultimate authority for obedience. Establish rules that teach God's expectations for life. Inspire obedience to God through knowledge and love for Him.

Parenting does not start with you. It starts with God. I cannot reiterate this point enough. If you do this and nothing else, it will revolutionize your parenting. In every interaction with your child, *appeal to God as the authority.* You, the parent, are only the temporary instrument of His authority.

Don't obey me! Obey God!

When my kids start talking, the first verse I teach them is Psalm 24:1: "The earth is the Lord's, and all it contains, the world, and those who dwell in it." Someone once asked me why. They thought it was an odd verse to teach a two-year-old. It has nothing to do with behavior or the basic things we normally focus on with young kids. The first thing I want my children to know is that God is in charge.

He is the creator and authority over all. The foundation of all knowledge is that God exists.

I've illustrated it in our home with what I call the tower of authority. Authority is the power or right to give orders, make decisions, and enforce obedience. God created a progression of authority for the ordering and working of His creation. Genesis 1:28 says, "God blessed them; and God said to them, 'Be fruitful and multiply, and fill the earth, and subdue it; and rule over the fish of the sea and over the birds of the sky and over every living thing that moves on the earth.'" God made man to have authority over the animals and the earth.

Then God made families. He gives children to parents. Ephesians 6:1–2 says, "Children, obey your parents in the Lord, for this is right. Honor your father and mother (which is the first commandment with a promise)." Parents have the God-given authority over their children to raise and teach them. "Fathers, do not provoke your children to anger, but bring them up in the discipline and instruction of the Lord" (Ephesians 6:4).

God created other entities to organize society and create order, specifically the government and the church. As my children get older, we talk about these different levels of authority. God has given each entity and each tier of authority jurisdiction over a certain area. As different law enforcement has jurisdiction over specific people and areas, so do the entities God set up. They are all limited in their jurisdiction and accountable to God. Parents have jurisdiction over their children and the home. Church leadership has jurisdiction over its congregation and church resources. Governments have jurisdiction over the aspect of citizenry and national affairs. God is at the top and the ultimate authority over all. "But Peter and the apostles answered, 'We must obey God rather than men'" (Acts 5:29). Masters or employers have authority over workers and the jurisdiction of employment. We can use God's order to teach our children about authority, who to obey in each area of life, and who is responsible for decisions in each area.

What is the fear of the Lord?

In every area of life, God is the authority. He is the one to be feared. The beginning of instruction for children is to teach them the fear of the Lord (Proverbs 1:7). So what is the fear of the Lord? The *fear of the Lord is to know God's position versus my position and to respond appropriately.* God is holy; I am a sinner. God is powerful; I am weak. God is all-knowing; I am limited in my knowledge. When a person understands who God is and who they are, they understand that the correct response is obedience.

I am terrified of black widow spiders. A few years ago, one of our pastors got bit by one. He was a big man, and this little spider knocked him down and made him sick. I fear black widows because I know what they can do. I saw one in my house a few summers ago. I didn't cuddle it or try to scoop it up and put it outside. My response was to kill it immediately. We should teach and lead our children to respond to God according to the knowledge available about Him.

What knowledge do we have about God? He has revealed Himself in Scripture and nature and ultimately showed who He was in the person of His Son, Jesus Christ. Knowledge of God comes from…

1. Scripture
2. Nature/Creation (Romans 1:19–20, Psalm 19:1)
3. Jesus—the image of the invisible God (Colossians 1:15, John 1:14)

Step 1: Know God

To teach your kids about authority and obedience, start with teaching them about God. Read them stories that reveal God's character and works. Here are some suggestions:

- Read the account of creation and talk about what creation reveals about God.
- Read the stories of the patriarchs in Genesis: Abraham, Isaac, Jacob, and Joseph. Discuss what these stories tell us

about God. What did the men think about God? How did God talk to them? What was their response to God?
- Read Exodus and the story of the Israelites in the wilderness. What was important to God in these stories? What does it tell us about God?
- Read the account of Joshua taking the promised land. What was Joshua's response to God? What does God do for His people? What is He like in these stories?
- Read about Saul, David, Ruth, Esther, Nehemiah, Daniel, Jonah. Read each narrative asking, "What does it tell us about God? How do the characters respond to God?" This will lay a huge foundation for understanding who God is, how He deals with man, and how we are to respond to Him.
- Spend time in nature. What does it tell you about God?
- Spend time with animals. What do their habits and their connection to time and seasons tell you about God?

Inspire before you require

As I worked out in my living room one cold, wintry evening, I was listening to a podcast where a man the same age as I had started a ministry called Save the Storks. This organization uses mobile ultrasound units to reach women in crisis pregnancy. They help women see their unborn babies, and then they provide them with the resources and contacts that will help them carry their babies to term. As I heard Joe Baker tell his story, he inspired me to make my story.

Inspiration is when someone or something fills you with a desire to do something. It reaches the heart to cause change from the inside. Heart change will cause behavioral change that is lasting and authentic. As a parent, I am in it for the long haul. I want lasting, authentic change in my children, so I want to inspire my children with God.

When I was a kid living in Spain, my parents used to show the movie *Jesus* as an outreach in small Spanish towns. I remember the scene when Jesus asked the disciples to go out and fish again after they had been fishing all night. They were discouraged and tired.

They had been out all night and had caught nothing. Think about it in a modern setting. You are teaching all day, and your students aren't getting it. They all fail the test. Or you have been marketing your product, spending time, ideas, and effort to sell it, and no one buys it. You plant, care for, and harvest your fields, and nothing grows. You create a piece of art that you have put your heart into, and no one likes it. The disciples felt like that. They had worked all night and had gotten nothing. Then Jesus asked them to do it again. It is as if He was secretly saying, "Watch what happens when I am part of your work." So the disciples do what He asks. They cast their nets again, but this time, the fish pour in. Their nets are so full they call for more boats. Then as the excitement dies down, Peter realizes what happened. He doesn't say thank you or wow. His response is "Depart from me. I am a sinner." When the knowledge of who Jesus was sunk into Peter, his response was one of fear of God and an inadequacy of self in the presence of one so great.

That is not the end though. They sat down to eat, and Jesus asked Peter if he loved Him. Three times, Jesus asked Peter, "Do you love me?" Peter answered, "Yes." Jesus asked again, "Peter, do you love me?" "Yes," Peter replied once more. "Peter, do you love me?" Jesus asked a third time. And again, Peter said, "Yes." But Jesus wanted not just a verbal response but a response of action. *You saw how great I was, Peter. If you love me, you will feed my sheep.* Jesus called Peter from His knowledge of Him to love Him, to a response of obedience to Him. In John 14:15, Jesus said, "If you love Me, you will keep My commandments."

How do you inspire obedience in your child?

Use this progression: *know*, *love*, and *obey God*.

From the time your child is young, give them encounters with God. Show them how great, awesome, loving, just, and powerful God is. Read stories about God. Talk about God's attributes. Take a walk and talk about the Creator and His wonders. Read about people who followed God. Fill your children with the wonder and excitement of knowing someone so awesome. Be an example of how much you love God's Word, His creation, and His ways. Don't just talk about God when it is punishment or correction time, but talk about God in happy, joyous times and daily circumstances.

Step 2: Know God's expectations

Part of knowing God is knowing what pleases and displeases Him. I am a pleaser. One of the most frustrating things for me is when I don't have clear expectations. When a person in authority over me does not clearly let me know what they want from me, I feel lost and frustrated. I think most kids struggle with this also; they just don't know how to express it. God is clear about what He expects. We need not wonder or walk on eggshells to please Him. He is not moody, nor does He change His mind. His expectations were set forth from the beginning, and they were clear and easy to understand. First John 5:3 says, "For this is the love of God, that we keep His commandments; and His commandments are not burdensome." Therefore, we want to teach God's expectations.

A simple way to teach what God expects in your home is to make a list of rules. Remember, you are teaching about God, so rules should be what God expects. Proverbs is full of these. Proverbs 1 tells us four things a child needs to do:

1. Fear the Lord (know and obey God).
2. Listen.
3. Beware and avoid certain people.
4. Seek wisdom.

Some tips on making rules

As you make rules, here are some tips based on Scripture.
Rules apply in every place and with every group of people.
When my kids leave my home, I want them to see that the rules are still valid. They are God's rules for life. They are not Mom and Dad's rules. We are kind because God says to be kind. We listen because God says listening will give us wisdom. We are good stewards because God calls us to steward the things He has given us. These

rules apply everywhere, in every circumstance, and at any age. They apply in the home, at church, on the playground, in the workplace, and in the nursing home.

No convenience rules. Rules should be against sin.

By this, I mean that rules should not just be convenient for me, the parent. When you ask your kids not to do something because it bugs you, that is a convenience rule or a preference. Rules should be the same for the two-year-old as for the seventeen-year-old. God does not change our expectations of us. When we are not consistent with our expectations, we sow roots of bitterness in our children. Ephesians 6:4 contrasts exasperating our children with bringing them up in the discipline and instruction of the Lord (God's rules). Rules are consistent and clear because we take them from God's Word. I do not want my children to obey me because I say so. I want them to obey God through me as the instrument of authority God has placed over them.

Therefore, we have chosen rules in our home from God's Word. We desire for our kids to ultimately have a life of obedience toward God, not us.

1. Listen
2. Obey
3. Be kind
4. Be a good steward
5. Be thankful

Rules that are simple and positive. There are only five. We want them to be easily remembered. They apply everywhere we go. And note that they are positive. They include all the "do nots." Being kind includes "do not hit," "do not bite," "do not spit," "do not yell," "do not make ugly eyes," etc. This is where you will use the teaching and training verbs of 2 Timothy 3:16. Go over examples of the rules and practice what it looks like to do it and not to do it. In the section dealing with the youths, I will show you how we expand and go in-depth with the rules as the kids get older. We hold them to a higher level but with the same concepts.

Purpose

There is one more thing I want to show you in Proverbs. God does not only tell us what to do, but He explains to us why. Parents, you can follow God's example by explaining the reason for the rule. What benefit or blessing will your child get from following this rule? This differs from a reward like money or a sticker. You are telling them why this rule is good for life. Look at Proverbs 3. Along with the commands, a list of benefits is paired with them. There are nine sets of commands and reasons for them.

Command: Do not let kindness and truth leave you. Bind them around your neck and write them on the tablet of your heart.
Reason: For they will give you favor and good repute with God and man.

Command: Trust in the Lord with all your heart and lean not on your own understanding. In all your ways know Him.
Reason: He will make your paths straight.

Command: Do not be wise in your own eyes. Fear the Lord and turn away from evil.
Reason: For it will be healing to your body and refreshment to your bones.

Command: Do not fear the onslaught of the wicked.
Reason: The Lord is your confidence and will keep you from being caught.

Each command has a "so" or a "for" with it. God lovingly tells us why He wants us to do what He has asked. Most of the time, the reasons are for our own benefit. When we make rules for our children, we need to make sure that the rules have purposes and that the purpose is for their long-term benefit.

Another way to know God is to learn what He doesn't like. Proverbs mentions a list of abominations. An abomination is literally something that "stinks" to God. This is a fun visual for young children. Talk about things that smell bad, and then list things that stink to God. Proverbs 6:16–19 has a list that we have memorized in our home: "There are six things which the Lord hates, yes seven which are an abomination to Him: haughty eyes, a lying tongue, and hands that shed innocent blood, a heart that devises wicked plans, feet that run rapidly to evil, a false witness who utters lies, and one who spreads strife among brothers." If we fear and love God, we will not want to do these things.

Concluding prayer

> Dear Lord,
>
> The fear of You is the beginning of knowledge. It is the beginning of a life well lived. Help me to know You and to teach my children to know You. Help me to lead by making time to spend with You in Your Word and in Your creation. Help our minds to have a proper understanding of who You are and Your position of authority. Please help me to be an example of knowing You and Your ways. Help me to teach my children about You and Your expectations. Help me be an instrument of Your authority and establish clear rules derived from Your Word. As we know You, may our love for You grow and our response be obedience. Help me to teach these things to my children and to inspire a love for You. May I be the instrument that will lead them to ultimately obey You. In Jesus's name, amen.
>
> Verse to pray: Isaiah 40:12–31

Practical Proverbs for the family

The naive
- Memorize verses concerning God's character and His authority. Some good ones are Psalm 24:1, Genesis 1:1–2, and Philippians 2:3–11.
- Read stories that tell about God's character. The Old Testament is great! It is full of God's power and authority. What happens when men or nations (Israel) disobey God?

The youths
- Make a tower of authority using these verses. Who does God say should obey and submit to whom?

    o Romans 13:3–5, Hebrews 13:17
    o Romans 13:1–2
    o Exodus 20:12, Ephesians 6:1–3
    o Genesis 1:28

The wise
- Look up these verses. What do people do in response to the fear of the Lord?

    o Exodus 1:17
    o Exodus 14:31
    o 1 Samuel 11:7
    o Job 1:1
    o Nehemiah 5:5-9
    o Jonah 1:16
    o Malachi 2:4–6

Parent reflection and application: write rules for your family

Here are some guidelines for making family rules:
- From Scripture: What does God expect me to teach my children? What does God require?
- Clear, positive, and simple: Children should be able to answer the question, "What do your parents expect from you?"
- Check that your rules are not for convenience but to please God.

Rules/guidelines in your family

1.
2.
3.
4.
5.

CHAPTER 3

The Fear of the Lord (Part 2)— Reproof

> Turn to my reproof, behold, I will pour out my spirit on you;
> I will make my words known to you.
>
> —Proverbs 1:23

Principle: Reproof and correction bring life and restoration. Consequences are given to protect one from the damages of sin and to deter one from sinning more.

Children will not always obey the rules. Out of necessity, a process is needed to deal with rule-breaking. Fortunately, God has laid that out in His manual. At the beginning of Proverbs in chapter 1, verse 23, wisdom cries out, "Turn to my reproof, Behold, I will pour out my spirit on you." Wisdom is crying out to the naive and foolish. She calls them to listen to her reproof, turn from their ways, and follow her. Reproving is not fun! To reprove means to convict of wrong and convince of the right. There is an aspect of arguing a case and proving that the right way is better. Parents, your biblical wisdom matters. You are to convince your kids of the right way. When they are wrong, you bring them back to the right way by convincing them of the better way—God's way. Reproof is needed to gain wisdom. If you want your children to avoid terror, calamity, distress, and anguish, we must be the Holy Spirit's instrument of reproof (Proverbs 1:24–33).

What is the purpose of reproof?

Sin has bad consequences. It costs time and energy. It hurts people. It breaks trust and damages relationships. It leads to want and need. It can cause physical damage to ourselves, others, and property. Above all, sin displeases God, and He wants us to avoid it and get rid of it.

God gives consequences so that sin will be avoided and not "cost" us so much. God designed parents to help their children when they sin by giving them short-term, temporary consequences. These consequences help teach children that sin is to be avoided. While our children are under our protection, they can sin and have consequences that will not affect them for a lifetime.

Most sins have natural consequences. To teach our children not to live in sin, we want to establish temporary unpleasantness in exchange for a longer-lasting consequence. Let me give some examples:

1) Your five-year-old child punches their sibling. In your home, they will receive a consequence for this. If your twenty-five-year-old son punches someone, he can be arrested and charged with assault. He will likely pay fees and have the incident put on his record.
2) Your child repeatedly does not get his homework done. He will get a bad grade in class. He may even have to repeat the class for incomplete work. If your adult child is in the workplace and repeatedly not getting his work done, the boss fires him. He has a mortgage, bills, and two young children to support and is out of work. The consequences are a lot more severe and long-lasting. God, in His merciful design, wants parents to teach children these things in the home where consequences are temporary and less severe.

Restorative consequences

Proverbs only speaks of one unnatural consequence: the rod. The other consequences are natural. There are natural rewards for following God. Likewise, there are bad consequences for not following God's rules. God demonstrates this principle in the Old Testament law. When someone sinned and broke the law, they were to restore damages to the person injured and sacrifice to God to restore the relationship with Him. In addition, it is interesting to note that Israel did not have jails. Consequences should be restorative to the damage caused by the sin. Here are some examples of consequences when the rules are broken in our home.

Be kind. Proverbs 19:5 says that kindness is attractive. When you are not kind, you lose friends or closeness and trust in a relationship. If your unkindness attracts the wrong people, you will have even more consequences. When one of our children lies, we let them know they are destroying trust. Losing trust will cause them to have less independence.

Be a good steward. When our children do not take care of themselves, their things, or our home, they lose the privilege of using and having things. If they do not do chores correctly, they must practice them more or do additional ones. If they cannot steward their body by the foods they eat or spending time outside, we monitor their schedule and habits more. In essence, they lose independence. When one of my sons was two, he wanted to sit at the table like a "big boy" instead of sitting in his high chair. When he got up from the table repeatedly and wouldn't eat his food, we put him back in the high chair, and he lost independence. He did not like that, so he learned to stay seated and eat his food.

Be thankful. We have an understanding in our home that when you are not thankful, you are showing you did not enjoy or appreciate something. If you did not enjoy or appreciate it, then you must not want to repeat it or have more of the same. If my kids do not show gratitude, say for going to a birthday party or having a treat, they will get it less often because I understand from their behavior that it was not enjoyed or appreciated.

Obey. Disobedience is the one thing we have additional, unnatural consequences for. Obedience is the priority and encompasses all rules. It also includes fear or respect for authority. Disobedience is serious because we cannot protect them if they do not obey. Our boys have to obey quickly, completely, and cheerfully with the answer of "Yes, Mom" or "Yes, Dad." When it is not done the right way, they must practice obeying correctly. They are asked to respond without whining, arguing, or complaining. They will need to repeat the task if it is not done completely.

What does Proverbs say about the rod?

First, Proverbs only mentions the rod eight times. Because of this, I think we can conclude that it is a minor part of reproof. Our first step should be to help convict them of wrong and convince them of right. Second, half of the time the rod is mentioned, it is in the context of using it with a fool. Sometimes, our children act foolish, so the rod should be used when foolishness is at its height. Proverbs 10:13 says, "On the lips of him who has understanding, wisdom is found, but a rod is for the back of him who lacks sense." If we can converse and get an understanding, then the rod is not needed.

The rod was a thin stick like a reed used to direct animals in the right path or keep them from danger. Psalm 23:4 says, "Your rod and Your staff, they comfort me." A shepherd would use a rod to direct his sheep to the right path or keep them from danger. The rod sometimes had a ball at the end with spikes on it. The shepherd would use it to nudge the sheep's hooves. This would redirect the sheep toward the correct path and keep them off the way that was dangerous. It caused minor pain, but the purpose was to protect and redirect from major danger.

Purpose of the rod

God has implemented and allowed consequences to deter us from sin because He is good and does not want us to live in its consequences. The rod is one temporary consequence. The purpose of the rod is to save the child, to give life. Proverbs 23:13–14 says that the rod will not bring death. In other words, it is not to beat the child and cause permanent damage.

When a young child sins, sometimes, the parent feels the consequence of shame and embarrassment from the offended party. For example, my kids have more than once made me late by throwing a fit right when we were about to leave the house. They cannot realize that being late for something is a bad habit. The rod gives an immediate consequence for a child who cannot understand the long-term consequences or the consequences that others will pay for him. You are purposefully giving a physical punishment that will not be lasting. The physical part is important because sin has physical consequences. Sin brings shame and guilty emotions that manifest themselves in physical forms such as fatigue, anxiety, depression, and so on. Many sins between people are physical and violent. Sins toward ourselves, such as laziness, gluttony, and drunkenness, bring physical consequences to our bodies. Sin is so physical in the consequences that it ultimately brings physical death (Romans 3:23).

Here are some tips when using the rod:

- Use it with younger children because they are foolishly naive.
- Use it with younger children when the natural consequence is not something they can understand.
- Use it for foolish behavior.
- Using the rod should not give a child permanent or even semipermanent physical, emotional, or relational damage.
- Never use it in anger. When used in anger, you are the fool.
- Do not use the rod if you do not consciously and affectionately show your child love through touch, such as hugs, kisses, holding, etc.

A child who has been abused rarely misbehaves because he is being foolish. He misbehaves because he likely has not been instructed or experienced the love of protection from his authority. These things must be met first and firmly established.

Restorative reproof

Your child needs one of two things: either witnessing or discipleship. Do you look at your child as someone who needs Jesus as much as the person down the street or down the hall from you at work? Your children are born lost and will perish without God. You, the parent, are the first preacher they get. Once your child becomes a believer, you are their discipler. Who else will you have more time with, more conversation with, more opportunity to show daily, real-life examples of a follower of Christ? You are like the Jesus they walk around with daily. Yes, it is a high calling! But remember, ask for wisdom and the Holy Spirit's help. You are doing God's work. *If your children are unbelievers, witness to them. If your children are believers, disciple them.*

If we fear the Lord and recognize Him for the ultimate authority He is, if the rules we live by come from God, then when disobedience occurs, it is an affront to God's rules, authority, and position. Psalm 51:4 says, "Against Thee, Thee only, have I sinned, And done what is evil in Thy sight." In practice, this means that the child has offended God and needs to rectify his or her relationship with God first. As a parent, I am the middleman between God and my child. I communicate God's position and His expectations (the rules). I am to help my child and their relationship with God.

When one of God's rules is broken, go through these steps:

- *Which expectation of God was not met?*

    When your child disobeys, ask which one of God's rules he or she broke. If you catch yourself saying things like, "I can't believe you are doing this again," "You are making me angry," or "I have told you not to do that," every one of those statements is about you, the parent. Sin needs to be about the child's relationship with God first. I am the middleman until they are old enough to deal with God on their own. Your statements should be, "You sinned," "You broke one of God's rules, that is called sin," or "This is not pleasing to God." Name the sin as the Bible names it.

- *Lead the child to confess*

    Help your child name the sins such as disobedience, unkindness, bad stewardship, angry eyes, lying, and planning evil. You want to lead him or her to confess. Do not list all the bad things they did. The goal is that they see their need for Jesus. Ask questions such as, "What did you do?" If they do not admit it, make the question easier for them to answer. "I saw you hit your brother when you were mad. Is that what happened?" "Did you hit?" "I think you lied. Is that true?" Confess means agree with. We help our children in their relationship with God when they know God and His expectations and can agree with God.

Here are some more tips:

- Don't let them retell the whole story.
- Let them express how they feel hurt. (It is human nature to want to be understood.)
- Don't let them give excuses for sin. ("He made me do it. He did it first.") Sin is serious. Jesus was nailed to the cross for sin.
- Don't let them hide or cover it up by lying. This adds more sin to the first sin, and then there is more to confess, ask forgiveness for, and restore.
- Don't let them blame others or circumstances for sin. We are responsible for ourselves and our choices, no matter the circumstances or the people. God calls us to do the right thing regardless of the situation or the other person involved.

Give established consequences

Here, you bring in whatever consequences you have established in your home. They should be clear and consistent. The ultimate consequence of sin is a broken relationship with God.

The solution

There is a solution for sin. Every instance of disobedience is an opportunity to show the plan of salvation. When your child sins, has admitted it, and you have given consequences, you can remind them of the good news that Jesus paid for our sins. Jesus forgives and helps us not to do it again by having His Holy Spirit live in us. Either ask the child or tell them how to do it correctly the next time. Always bring them back to the right way (2 Timothy 3:16).

If you have established rules in your home that are from God and not your own convenience, this process will work well. If you have established your preferences as rules, it will be hard to bring God into the picture.

Hope of restoration

According to the Bible, the purpose of discipline or reproof is to save the soul. Proverbs 19:18 says, "Discipline your son while there is hope, And do not desire his death." Discipline's purpose is to expose sin, the problem, so your child can have a relationship with God and have life.

The process takes time. This is not a quick go-in-the-corner-and-have-a-time-out.

Here is a review:

Process when rules are broken
Step 1: Identify the sin.
Step 2: Lead them to confess.
Step 3: Give out natural and restorative consequences.
Step 4: Remind of the solution Jesus provided.
Step 5: Do the work of restoration and reconciliation of relationship.

I am not perfect. I have yelled at my kids, removed them from the situation, and avoided places when they would not behave. When I do it God's way, the results are way better. Even when I don't see immediate results, I have peace that I am following God. When I resort to my ways, I feel discouraged and frustrated, and so do my children.

These are all things I have done that don't accomplish a restoration of my relationship with God or bring my children back to God's way:

1. *Telling children what they did was wrong with no instruction, no teaching, and no practice of correct behavior.* This is condemnation.
2. *Lecturing about how inconvenient it is for you.* Example: "I can't believe you would do this again. You make it so hard for us to do anything fun. Now I have to…" This is condemnation again.
3. *Removing kids out of the situation or avoiding situations.* Examples: "We can't go to that restaurant because you don't behave." This is avoiding the sin problem and the heart. There is no teaching.
4. *Time-outs.* Instead of making time-outs a consequence or bad thing, make it a good thing, a way to take the time to control anger and outbursts. God commands us to be still so this can be a positive experience.
5. *Yelling.* The anger of man does not accomplish the righteousness of God.
6. *Be careful of rewards that modify behavior, such as stickers, money, and points for a prize.* I love rewarding my kids for doing something well, but don't make this your focus. Sometimes, doing the right thing does not bring you an earthly reward. (See examples in Scripture such as Joseph, Paul, and Daniel.) God's rewards are eternal and longer lasting (a clean conscience, trust, faithfulness to God, integrity, character). They are better than man's rewards.

Concluding prayer

> Dear Lord,
>
> You are holy, and we are sinful, yet You love us so much. You care for us and don't want us to live in sin because its consequences are detrimental to us. Thank You for providing a way to guide us away from sin. Thank You for providing Your Son who took care of sin. I even thank You for the consequences that deter us from sin. Help me to follow Your ways and teach my children so we avoid sin and can live in the benefits of Your blessings. Please help me to apply consequences correctly for my children. Give me wisdom to know what to use and how to use it. Help me to remember that reproof is to give life by convicting of wrong and convincing of right. May I be an instrument that will lead my children to follow You. In Jesus's name, amen.
>
> Verse to pray: Psalm 1

Practical Proverbs for the family

The naive
- Memorize verses that tell of the things that are an abomination to God, such as Proverbs 6:16–19.
- Read stories that show there are consequences to sin (Cain killing Abel, Joshua and Jericho, Ai after the sin of Achan, Saul's disobedience to God, Jonah, etc.).

The youths
- List the abominations (things that are stinky to God) and talk about them.

- Read stories that show that doing the right thing may not bring earthly rewards. Read the stories of Joseph, Daniel, Shadrach, Meshach, Abednego, Paul, and Jesus. How were these men rewarded for right conduct? What eternal, lasting rewards did they get?

The wise
- Read through several prophets. Look at three things: what are the sins God lists that Israel committed? What will be the consequence for them? How does God show His love and mercy and future restoration of Israel? (For example: Micah, Zechariah, Amos, and Zephaniah.)

Parent reflection

- Write out your own steps to go through when a child breaks the rules. Think of verses that will help you remember them.
- Do your own research and make your own decisions about the rod. What does Proverbs and Psalms say about it?

    - Proverbs 10:13
    - Proverbs 13:24
    - Proverbs 22:8
    - Proverbs 22:15
    - Proverbs 23:13–14
    - Proverbs 26:3
    - Proverbs 29:15
    - Psalm 23:4
    - Psalm 89:30–33

My conclusions about the rod

CHAPTER 4

Listen, My Son (Part 1)— Children

> Listen, my son, to your father's instruction, And do not ignore your mother's teaching; For they are a graceful wreath for your head, And necklaces for your neck.
>
> —Proverbs 1:8–9

Principle: Listening is a growing skill.

God has given us two ears and one mouth. I wonder if He intended that we listen twice as much as we talk. The second pair of verses I teach my boys is Proverbs 1:8–9. Can you picture a two-year-old acting out, putting a necklace around her neck and a crown on her head? Listening adorns you. It makes you attractive. It gives you rewards.

Proverbs 2 gives us the method to attain the things that Proverbs 1 lists as the goal. Do you remember the seven things that are the purpose of Proverbs? Here they are again:

- to know wisdom and instruction
- to discern the sayings of understanding
- to receive instruction in wise behavior, righteousness, justice, and equity
- to give prudence to the naive

- to give youths knowledge and discretion
- for the wise to hear and increase in learning
- to understand a proverb, a figure, the words of the wise, and their riddles

Here is the method:
Proverbs 2:1–5 says the following:

> My son, if you will receive my words and treasure my commandments within you, make your ear attentive to wisdom, incline your heart to understanding; for if you cry for discernment, lift your voice for understanding; if you seek her as silver and search for her as for hidden treasures; then you will discern the fear of the lord and discover the knowledge of god.

"Hear, O Israel!" The call to listen and hear is common in the Bible. The fear of the Lord is the beginning of knowledge, but listening is the beginning skill to get it. Learning, loving, and following God all depend on listening.

In this chapter, we will talk about the first skill we should teach our children, and that is to listen. Proverbs mentions some form of listening twenty-one times. Sometimes, the concept is mentioned as listening or hearing; other times, it is mentioned with the phrases "Pay attention" or "Incline your ear." I love the phrase "Incline your ear." It literally means to bend your ear toward. Picture your children bending their ears toward you, God, or wisdom. What a blessed thing to see!

What children need to do

Childhood is a time to learn. It is that one season when all our energy is devoted to learning. Once one becomes an adult, learning continues, but it is not our main job in life. There are other things to do, such as making money, paying bills, raising kids, and keeping a home.

We will see in Proverbs how the skill of listening grows as a child matures. Listening itself is an action that becomes so active it leads to searching and yearning. Parents are to guide their children into learning this skill.

Raising children involves two sets of hearts: the parents' and the child's. In this chapter, we will look at the responsibility of the child, and in the next, we will look at the responsibility of the parent. As a mom, I tend to beat myself up and blame myself when my kids do something wrong. I'm sure many moms can relate to this. Yes, my kids reflect me, but there is also an element of their responsibility. They have a will that makes choices. They have a heart response to God also.

Here is a child's to-do list:

Receive. A child is to *receive*. Stop for a minute and think about a child's birthday. My boys love watching people open presents on their birthdays. They do not want to leave a birthday party before the birthday child opens the gifts. Imagine a child at her birthday party. All the children are sitting down to see what their friends will get. The gifts are all piled around the child, who is about to begin opening presents. But the birthday child gets up, screams, and runs away. He does not want his presents. He will not receive them. When children do not listen, they are like that birthday child. Children are to receive their parents' *commands, teachings, instructions, and sayings* (more on these four things in the next chapter).

How can parents encourage reception? By being proactive, not reactive. Help children receive instruction before they are in trouble. A parent's duty is to first cultivate a heart that is willing to receive. Fostering a receptive heart in our child requires two things. The first is gentleness in our instruction and interactions. Ephesians 6:4 tells fathers not to exasperate their children. One of the best ways to be gentle with your child is to preempt problems by teaching and training before there is a problem to address. Teach your child the expectations ahead of time. When you teach when there is no problem, you are not angry or frustrated, and your child has not put up a wall of defense.

Practice and train for reception. Since listening or receiving is a skill, we will teach this a little differently than we would a fact or knowledge. An athlete practices a skill repeatedly. A musician practices scales or chord positions repeatedly. We practice correct behavior, attitudes, and responses repeatedly.

Here are some practical ways to train children to receive instruction:

- *Come when called.* We play the name game. They pretend they are playing or doing something, and I call their name. They are to come immediately.
- *Respond and acknowledge they heard a command or instruction.* When I tell my children something, they must acknowledge they heard me by saying, "Yes, ma'am," or repeat what I said.
- *Obey a command by playing "Mommy says," like Simon says.* Make it fun!
- *Look at someone's eyes when being spoken to.*
- *Read someone's facial expressions and feelings.* Play a game where you guess someone's emotion by their facial expression.
- *Ask questions to clarify.* Teach your kids to ask questions when given a command or instruction they may not understand.
- *Listen with their full body.* We call it "soldier listening." It involves "eyes watching, ears listening, mouth quiet, and body still." They stand at attention like a soldier.
- *Show interest in someone or something with body language.* When someone talks, we stop what we are doing and show we want to hear what they say.
- *Rephrase what someone says.* For example, "This is what you mean…"
- *Summarize what someone said.* "So the main thing I hear you communicating is…"

Identify settings and situations where listening is important.

- *Bible reading time where you learn from God's Word.* What does your body behavior look like?
- *Prayer time where we talk to God and listen to Him.* Close your eyes to picture Jesus in heaven before God's throne. Read a passage like Revelation 4 to show who you are talking to.
- *Dinner time where we talk and listen to each other.* How do we take turns to have a conversation? What level of voices should we have?
- *School time where we listen to learn.*
- *Instruction time, after we have disobeyed and need to listen to corrective instruction.*

Treasure. A child is to *treasure*. A treasure is valuable. Before information was backed up in clouds, if you asked any mom what she would grab if her house was on fire, the answer was usually "My photos." We all value something, whether it is memories, time with family, days off, possessions, entertainment, people, or money. What we value determines how we act. Valuing the photos determines the action of getting them from the fire. Parents need to cultivate in their children a heart that would treasure God's words and our words. We are cultivating not only hearts that will receive what we say but also hearts that will treasure or value what God says.

Here is a little experiment you can do with your kids. Ask them to tell you something you say a lot. Is what you say worth treasuring? Parents need to give treasures! What we say should impart worth that lasts a lifetime. I would advise that we follow the example in Proverbs by making our words short, repetitive, in the normal course of life, and based on God's way.

How can parents encourage treasuring? By making what we say attractive with love and gentleness.

A child will not treasure commands yelled at them. A child will not treasure words spoken in annoyance, vengeance, or frustration. We are to speak so our words will be treasured. Do you remember words that made a difference to you? Words you will not forget but that you keep with you as a treasure? We are to speak in love and gentleness with the idea that we are doing it as representatives of God. We are the first picture our children see of God. We are to make their hearts ready to treasure God's truth.

In love. Ephesians 4:15 says, "But speaking the truth in love, we are to grow up in all aspects into Him."

With gentleness. Proverbs 15:1 says, "A gentle answer turns away wrath, but a harsh word stirs up anger."

Firm but not harsh. Ephesians 6:4 says, "Fathers, do not provoke your children to anger, but bring them up in the discipline and instruction of the Lord."

Practice and train for treasuring by showing value with repetition and consistency. Inconsistency and lack of clarity cause confusion, frustration, and resentment. Solomon repeats the principles in Proverbs over and over. He says the same things many times and in different ways. For example, anger is mentioned over eighty times. We need to be patient and repeat the same truths in order to show our children by repetition and consistency what is valued and worth saying.

Both of these first two commands, to receive and treasure, talk about what the child does in response to the parent. This is the first stage or foundation. You are the main instructor and teacher in their life. Solomon says his son is to receive his words and treasure his commands. We will see now that the next two commands change in the level of responsibility to the child and what the child is to listen to.

Make ear attentive. Is your child ready to listen when you speak? Ready to hear when wisdom is to be dispensed? At the gym where my boys do gymnastics, there is a vending machine. For some reason, it is so appealing to them to get a candy bar at the vending machine. I have told them they could get more for their money at the store, but they like putting in the money, choosing something, and having it dispensed. It is an exciting thing they look forward to at the end of practice. A child should be ready to get instruction or wisdom when a parent or other authority speaks as if it is a treat to be dispensed.

How can parents encourage attentiveness? By identifying those of authority who have knowledge and wisdom to dispense.

One thing that I teach in our home is that when Mom, Dad, or other authorities speak, such as a coach, teacher, or pastor, the child is to act like it is an alarm going off. Warning, warning, warning! An alarm is sounding! Important information for life is about to be given by this person! Instruction for the right way to go in a math problem, the parallel bars, or how to clean the bathroom is being dispensed! Someone in authority is about to give a nugget for life. I better stop what I am doing and be attentive!

Practice and train for attentiveness by pointing out people and situations that will dispense valuable knowledge.

We should have regular people and resources in life that we know will dispense treasures of knowledge for us—the Bible, a sermon, church service, grandparents, books, people with character, and so on. Teach children where good sources of knowledge and wisdom are so that they will be ready to listen to these. On the other hand, help them see places and people that are not valuable for knowledge and wisdom.

Incline their heart to understanding. Do you notice the heart is mentioned here? The heart is the whole being. Picture a person bending their whole self toward understanding. We will talk more about this word "understanding" later on. Proverbs 18:2 says, "A fool does not delight in understanding, but only in revealing his own mind." One whose heart is inclined toward understanding wants to know more than he wants to tell. Here are some questions to ask:

Does your child want to understand another person in a disagreement? Do they want to know why that person did what they did? Is their attitude one of trying to comprehend what you were explaining? Do they have an attitude of arrogance or humility toward you? Do they treat you like you are an annoyance when you talk? Do they roll their eyes? Do they understand their position of submission to you under God's authority in the way they treat you, look at you, and respond to you? Is their heart bent toward understanding God's ways?

This is a process where we teach our children to think bigger than themselves. They are trying to understand God's ways. One will start to see another's perspective. They are beginning to see the reasoning for a command given. Their heart is at a new stage of humility and understanding. A teachable heart becomes more evident.

How can parents encourage inclining the heart? By the above steps and prayer.

Because this involves the heart, I don't think there is much a parent can do other than lay the foundations of the previous stages and pray for teachableness. Someone who inclines their heart to understanding is someone whose heart has been worked on by God. *Don't forget to pray for your kids! Here are some practical ways to pray for your children:*

One thing I did when I was pregnant was to ask God for a verse or passage to pray over each of my children. Each child has a verse that God gave me to regularly pray for them. It is like their theme verse. It has been neat to see how each verse is related to their personalities. One of my boys is timid. He fears new situations and changes. In God's sovereignty, He gave me the verse John 16:33 for him: "These things I have spoken to you, so that in Me you may have peace. In the world you have tribulation, but take courage; I have overcome the world." This boy regularly needs courage. God knew this boy would need this verse even when he was in the womb.

Cry for discernment and lift your voice for understanding. My boys loved playing with balloons when they were preschool age. Inevitably, someone's balloon would get popped, and they would cry over it. We cry over what matters to us, what we define as important, and what is needed or lost. Here, Proverbs tells us to cry for discernment and lift our voices for understanding. Are we so desperate for the ability to judge between right and wrong—discernment—that we cry for it? Do we teach our kids that this ability is worth tears? God desires our hearts and that of our kids to cry for what matters to Him and what He says we need.

In addition, we need understanding. The word for "lift" in this verse means "to give" or "put." The word in Hebrew is *Nathan*. My brother's name is Nathan, and one of my son's middle name is

Nathaniel. So I automatically knew this word meant "gift." What it is saying is to give our voice understanding. What we have heard, received, treasured, and inclined our hearts toward now comes out in our voice for others to hear.

Seek her and search for her as silver or treasure. We have a tradition of watching the movie *National Treasure* around the Fourth of July. In the movie, the characters are searching for treasure. But throughout the search, there are a lot of dead ends. A child at this stage can begin to recognize the dead ends of where they will not get wisdom. Further, it also means they are learning to prioritize. When seeking something, you choose not to do other things. The characters in *National Treasure* were so determined to seek the treasure that it was a priority over breaking the law and risking prison time.

If we analyze the list, we will see that the responsibility grows. It starts with the more passive commands to receive and treasure. Then the action begins to make the ear attentive and incline their hearts. Finally, they are moved to action by crying and seeking to learn. This is not only a picture of the growing responsibility of the child but of the growing passivity of the parent. We start with words that the child will receive and treasure. Our role is active, and theirs is more passive. Moreover, they are like that sponge that soaks in everything we teach them. Therefore, we are to prepare the heart so that it is open to receive and treasure.

Later, they must initiate this quest for God's way of life. They must not only receive and treasure it but be attentive and lean toward God's way so that faith and a relationship with God become their own. Parents can help them by slowly letting go and letting them develop their own relationship with God. By the time they have grown in these skills, their heart should be ready to seek God more independently.

As can be seen by this section, one of the main themes in Proverbs is the ability to listen. To demonstrate, read Proverbs 1:20–33, where wisdom calls to men. A book about wisdom requires a discussion on the means to get wisdom. That means is through listening and teachability.

Concluding prayer

Dear Lord,

Thank You for giving us so much instruction and guidance. Help my children to listen and receive instruction. Help their hearts to be teachable, to receive and treasure instruction. Help them to be attentive and cry for and seek Your wisdom. Help me to be an instrument to pass on Your truth and wisdom to them. Help me also to be teachable and listen to You so I may continue to grow as I teach the future generation of You. In Jesus's name, amen.

Verse to pray: Psalm 34:11

Practical Proverbs for the family

The naive
- *Games and fun practice*

    - Come up with your own phrase for good listening.
    - Practice facial expressions by playing the face game. (Child guesses what mood or feelings you have.)
    - Listening is paying attention to tone and reading body language and facial expression, not just hearing words. Play the voice game and say the same phrase in different tones and have them guess how you are feeling based on the tone.
    - Look and listen game: name things in the room with the pronouns "this and that" and "here and there" to demonstrate that listening requires looking.

- *Be still and listen.* Stop and listen. Do nothing else. Listen to music, stories, or podcasts where there are no visuals.

- *Make conversation rules.* For example:

    o   Take turns to talk
    o   Respond to others
    o   Ask questions
    o   Restate

- Have conversation time. Ask interesting questions at the dinner table or before bed and practice these rules. Give everyone an assignment based on something they like. For example, "Micah, tell me how to do a roundoff back handspring." Others can ask questions about it. Then someone else should restate by summarizing what he said.

The youth
- Continue to train for the skills of a good listener.
- Look and identify body language and facial expressions.
- Seek first to understand, then to be understood (from *7 Habits of Highly Effective People*).

    Put yourself in their shoes. Imagine how they feel. Imagine what has happened to them. Imagine their life and situation. Think about why they act that way or say those things. What is their motivation? Think of their perspective and seek to understand them before you try to get them to understand your side.
- Have kids at this stage read their Bibles on their own and develop their own quiet time and relationship with God. Give them a journal to write down prayers.

The wise
- Why is listening so important? How does it help our learning, relationships, and stewardship?
- Read about these examples of good or poor listeners in the Bible:

- Jesus and Nicodemus (John 3:1–21)
- Job's friends (Job 16:1–8)
- David when confronted by Nathan (2 Samuel 12:1–14)

What can you learn from them?

Parent reflection and application

- How would you define the concept of listening, receiving, paying attention, and inclining your ear from what you have read in Proverbs?
- Practice with your kids.
- Stop when your children talk to you. Don't make them say your name several times. Bend down and give them your full attention. Don't interrupt!
- Check your heart and listening skills. These are for us too!
- How will you practice and teach your kids to listen? Work on one thing this week that concerns improving listening. Then reflect on how it went.

CHAPTER 5

Listen, My Son (Part 2)— Parents

> Hear, O sons, the instruction of a father, And give attention that you may gain understanding, For I give you sound teaching; Do not abandon my instruction. When I was a son to my father...then he taught me and said to me, "Let your heart hold fast to my words; Keep my commandments and live."
>
> —Proverbs 4:1–4

Principle: Parents must have a word for their children to listen to.

Parent responsibility

Proverbs, in its discussion on listening, gives the commands to the children but, in the process, assumes that parents have something to say that is worth their children listening to. We've already looked at the progression that children should go through. Now let's look at what parents need to do. There are four things that Solomon told his son to listen to.

What a mom and dad need to have

A father and mother must have four things: commandments, teachings, instructions, and sayings. Let's look at the difference between these so that we know what we are to be saying to our kids.

Parents must impart *commandments*. Commands are not rules! The word for "commandment" means a charge. It is giving or appointing responsibility. I command you to be in charge of this. Think of it as an army officer having command over his troops. As your children grow each year, they should have additional responsibilities. You are raising adults, not children. The goal is independence.

Our family does Christmas movie marathons. Every year, we watch the movie *Home Alone*. In the beginning, the family is getting ready to go to Paris for the holidays, and eight-year-old Kevin's mom tells him to go pack his suitcase. Kevin freaks out and goes around asking everyone for help. When my kids are three, I teach them how to pack a suitcase. It is a list of needed clothes and the items you use every day in your routine. The list has pictures so that any three-year-old can see three shirts, find them in the drawer, and put them in a suitcase. I check to make sure they do not forget anything, but they usually don't. Children are a lot more capable of responsibility than we think they are. Likewise, one thing my father-in-law did for his sons' birthdays was to allow them to choose to do something by themselves that they could not do before. My husband said that one year, he asked to cross the street by himself. His dad taught him how to do it safely. He then had a charge over crossing the street.

This is important, especially if you have boys. Men want to be strong and independent. We cannot baby young men and treat them like they are incapable. We are to give them command of more things and charge them with more to protect, defend, and manage. When leaving for a trip or when Tim is out of town, my boys all have charge of locking up the house and making sure things are in order so that our house is secure and guarded. I love hearing my little men tell me everything's safe and ready.

Parents, you are raising men and women who will someday have their own homes and families, so you must give them opportunities to practice where it is safe to make mistakes. Give them charge over more chores. Make them your partner in fixing the fence, mowing the lawn, the grocery budget, the meal plan, baking a birthday cake, writing a check for the bills, reading to their younger sibling, etc. *Give* them *command*.

Parents must have teachings. The word for "teachings" in Proverbs is Torah, the word for law. It comes from the verb *yarah,* which means to throw or shoot, as an archer. You, the parent, are to shoot them toward the right path. You are to aim them in the correct way—God's way—with your teachings.

God's laws were not just a list of requirements to follow Him. God's laws are about how to live life. The Bible is a book about God's ways for everything. It tells us how to live successfully in family, health, finances, relationships, spirituality, vocations, politics/law, and education. The Bible talks about every aspect of life and every sphere of governance and relationships.

As a parent, you are to teach your children about God's way in every area of life. Proverbs 10–31 tells about many of these *teachings* or ways. So hold on, and we will get to them! The best way to know what to teach your kids is to read the Bible! The more you read it, the better you will know how to direct them in God's ways.

Parents must have instructions. Instructions are what we think of as discipline. They are the chastening or correction. Consequently, instruction is usually not fun. In Scripture, instruction is always associated with God. This puts fear in me. As a parent, I am God's instrument for my child's instruction, so I better make sure I am submitting and listening to God.

Proverbs give us the image that life is a path. If teachings are God's way of life from Scripture, then instructions are the discipline and correction that help you get back on that path when you get off of it. It is easy to think of this when correcting a math problem, a skill in a sport, or playing an instrument. The instructor usually says, "This is not how you do it. It is done this way. Now practice." Likewise, this same process can be used for teaching God's way.

This is not how you treat others, deal with anger, take care of your room, or talk to me.

Let me show you how to treat others, deal with anger, take care of your room, or talk to me.

Now practice how to treat others, deal with anger, take care of your room, or talk to me.

Parents must have sayings. These are those things you say repeatedly. Sayings are short phrases that simply communicate truth. In addition, the sayings are your unique way of communicating with your children. These are the things that your kids will remember, "My mom always used to say that to me." We have a list of our sayings framed in our home. Here are some of them:

"God's ways are always best and bring blessing."
"See a problem. Be a solution."
"Kindness is attractive" (Proverbs 19:22).
"A gentle answer turns away anger" (Proverbs 15:1).

My parents used to tell me during my teenage years, "Nothing good happens after midnight." It used to drive me crazy because I had the earliest curfew of any of my friends. At least, I thought so. But now as I look back, I know my parents were trying to protect me, and I am glad they did.

What will your kids say you always said?

Here is a review of the things parents need to have:

Commands	Teachings	Instructions	Sayings
This is what you are responsible for…	This is God's Way for…	This is how you… You need to work on…	Communicate clearly Small truths
These are my expectations of you… A charge	The Torah points toward God's ways	Practice this… Correction with explanation	A word or short phrase

Concluding prayer

> Dear Lord,
>
> Thank You again for guiding me in what I am to tell my children. Help me to establish clear commands or charges for them. Help me to learn Your ways so I can continually tell them about You. Help me to be a good instructor so I can explain and correct them well. And finally, help me to communicate truths clearly and simply with little sayings. I pray that they will keep these with them their whole life and that they will teach their children. May our family be one that carries on Your truths and ways for many generations. In Jesus's name, amen.

Verse to pray: Psalm 78:1–8

Parent reflection and application

- What commands or charges do you give your children?
- Set appropriate chores by age. Give children more charge as they grow.
- What teachings do you tell your children? Are you reading God's Word and learning His ways?
- What instructions do you give your children? Do you show them how to do things, whether being kind or making a meal?
- What are the sayings you want to be known for? What will your kids say all the time when they leave your home?

CHAPTER 6

Beware

> Do not let your heart turn aside to her ways, Do not stray into her paths. For many are the victims she has cast down, And numerous are all her slain.
>
> —Proverbs 7:25–26

Principle: There are certain characteristics in people that we need to beware of, for they will lead us into the wrong ways and, ultimately, death.

Within the first section of Proverbs, Solomon mentions watching out for those who would lead us astray. Solomon gives his son a warning against two types of people. He lists characteristics we can use to identify them in order to aid in discernment. He also gives us the consequences of joining them. First, in Proverbs 1:10–19, he warns against the sinner. Then in Proverbs 5 through 7, Solomon gives a warning about the adulterous woman.

The first person we are to beware of is simply referred to as the sinner. The father wants his son to be aware of the means the sinner uses to entice. The sinner will tempt the son with belonging. In this section, the sinner uses the pronouns "us" or "we" eight times. They are going to do these things together and share the wealth, spoil, and purse. When belonging is not achieved in the family, there will always be groups ready to accept those who have no place.

As well as belonging, the sinner is enticed with excitement and the rush of doing evil. They lie in wait and ambush. One of my sons and I talked about how sin is exciting. He admitted that sneaking around and doing the wrong thing can be exciting. Parents, we need to be honest with our kids that sin is attractive at first. There is an appeal to it, or no one would sin.

With belonging and excitement, the next caution is against violence. Proverbs 6:17 says that God hates the shedding of innocent blood. But these sinners prey on the innocent, an easy target. Our sin nature will not strive to do the hard work but will always try to find a shortcut. It is easier to physically hurt those weaker than us than to hold our power in check. I have five boys and regularly observe how my kids interact and play with others. We have a neighbor they often play with. This child is the same age as my older kids but will often take things and bother my youngest. He never has an issue with the older ones. It is easier to feel powerful and better about yourself when you can make someone weaker than you feel insignificant.

Finally, he tempts with material gain, wealth, spoil, and the purse. Greed is one of the simplest and most common temptations for doing evil. We will talk more about greed, wealth, and money in future chapters. To summarize, we need to teach our kids to watch out for someone who has rejected his family, likes the rush of evil or sin, is violent, and uses his power to abuse the innocent or those weaker than him.

Here is a list of things to beware of regarding the sinner:

Beware of their pleasures
- The rush and delight of evil
- Prey on the innocent or weak
- Easy gain of wealth

Beware of their values
- Belonging to a group
- Adventure at any cost
- Violence

The adulteress

The second passage, chapters 5 through 7, deals with the adulterous woman. Instead of appealing to belonging to a group, the adulteress uses different means. She wants to isolate the man. She wants to get him alone so she can tempt him with flattery and pleasure. She flatters and uses smooth speech to appeal to his pride or to the one who lacks self-esteem. She is cunning and persuasive. The adulterous woman is like a predator. She targets the weak, vulnerable man that she can catch easily. She gets him to follow her by enticing him with physical pleasures. In summary, teach your kids to watch out for a woman who wants to isolate, who flatters and uses her attractiveness as power.

Here is a list of things to beware of regarding the adulterous:

Beware of her speech	*Beware of her timing*	*Beware of the pleasures*
Hiding/covering up sin	Nighttime	Physical
Boisterous		Visual
Persuasive toward wrong		Pride coming from listening to flattery
Flattery		

One thing to note about the adulteress is the timing. She does her deeds at night. Our God is a God of light. Dark deeds are usually done in darkness. I tell my boys to watch how someone responds to confrontation or exposure to wrong. Do they make excuses and try to "hide" or cover up what has been brought to light? Excuses and lying are warning signs of someone who hides sin. This behavior is something we should beware of in friends and companions and even ourselves.

These two examples, the sinner and the adulteress, are pretty extreme. I think Solomon is giving simple examples that are easy for a young person to understand. Discernment is easier when there are extremes. It is also important to note that the passage of the adulteress is couched in figurative language that does mention aspects of sexual relationships. These passages would be important to return to as children are able to handle them.

Given these points, we can see that Proverbs emphasizes the skill of discernment. We have learned that the skill to be wise is to be teachable and listen. One aspect of wisdom is to discern right from wrong and those situations and people that will lead us to right or wrong. It is important to start early talking to your kids about people. These characteristics can help guide discernment. Talk about how and what people talk about. Do they try to make people laugh by being perverse or demeaning to others? Do they change what they say around different people? Are they flatterers? Are they always trying to persuade or convince you to do something wrong?

I have told my kids the story about someone I had a relationship with for over five years. This person wasn't the sinner or adulteress mentioned here, but their habits were worth noting. During this relationship, not once did I hear the person ask about me or another person. They always started and kept the conversation on themselves. I don't use the story to be judgmental but to illustrate to my kids to watch and observe people. This person ended up with a broken marriage. How much does someone listen versus talk? What do they talk about? Do they argue a lot? Do they have to be right? Do they have an attitude of gratitude or complaining? Are they always changing their mind? Do they follow through with what they say? Teach them to be people observers and listeners and to express what they see. One of my prayers for my boys is that they would find good friends and be the good friends that others can find.

The consequences

I mentioned before that sin is enticing. The pleasures and fulfillment are temporary, but the consequences are longer-lasting. We must teach our children to weigh the temporary pleasure against the long-term consequences. Solomon declares the consequences of joining the sinner and giving in to the adulterous as a path that always ends in death. You will give your best years and most strength to those who will use it and waste it. It is a one-way relationship with these people.

Death is the ultimate consequence of sin. Romans 6:23 says, "For the wages of sin is death, but the gift of God is eternal life in Christ Jesus our Lord." I think that beyond these examples given for discernment's sake, Solomon is emphasizing to his son that sin leads to death. These passages are opportunities to explain to our children the consequences of following a path of sin and the blessings of believing in Jesus and His work on the cross. Proverbs continues to mention the types of people and behaviors that lead to life and those that lead to death.

Concluding prayer

> Dear Lord,
>
> Help us to be discerning. Help me to recognize good and evil and to recognize people who run to good and evil. Help me to teach my children to discern the speech, the timing, the habits, and the values of those that will lead them away from You. The enemy is smart and wants my children. Help me to see the spiritual battle going on, to be on guard, and to realize that raising my kids is a battle. Give me Your strength and Your wisdom to raise them. Protect us from the evil one. In Jesus's name, amen.
>
> Verse to pray: 1 Peter 5:8

Practical Proverbs for the family

The naive
- Learn to identify these characteristics in characters in stories/literature. This is an easy first step where it is not personal, and we can be careful to learn not to judge others.

The youth
- Learn to identify these characteristics in people and beware of them. We always pray and love people. This is not to judge them but to be careful.

The wise
Have discussion:
- What are my personal areas of weakness and temptation?
- Be a people observer and listener, and express what you see and hear for the purpose of discernment, not judgment.

Parent reflection and application

- Pray for your kids, their friends, the influences, and their own weak areas of temptations.
- Pray that if your child joins the wrong people and behaviors, his/her sin is caught/brought to light right away.

Use this layout to pray for your kids.
    Child's name:
    Child's strength:
    Child's weakness:
    Area of temptation: What do they crave?
    Pray for the Holy Spirit to fill this weakness.
    Verse to pray for this child according to their needs:
    Pray for godly friends. Pray that my child will be a godly friend.

CHAPTER 7

Wisdom

> Trust in the Lord with all your heart and do not lean on your own understanding. In all your ways acknowledge Him, and He will make your paths straight.
>
> —Proverbs 3:5–6

Principle: The key wisdom is to be teachable. Wisdom is demonstrated through our character and our relationship to God and others.

Now we are at the fourth foundational teaching in Proverbs: wisdom. Wisdom is simply the skill of living well. Proverbs tells us how to get wisdom, what it looks like, where it is found, and why one should strive for it. The Hebrew word for wisdom entails three main concepts: skill, experience, and shrewdness.

In our society, we measure someone's ability by how many facts they can memorize and regurgitate on a test. The skills of managing relationships or time, good communication, discipline, dealing with conflict, and hard work are not ones we measure. There is a big difference between knowledge and wisdom. Knowledge is facts. Wisdom is the skill of using the facts. It comes from practice, time, and being a good judge of right and wrong that can be skillfully applied in different situations and with different people.

Key to wisdom

We have seen that to get wisdom, we have to listen and be willing to be corrected. "Turn to my reproof, Behold, I will pour out my spirit on you; I will make my words known to you" (Proverbs 1:23). The most obvious characteristic of a wise person is teachableness. Are you humble enough to be a lifelong learner and student of wisdom? Following God looks like being a student of His—a disciple. We are to learn about Him, His ways, and His desires. This means we turn from our ways and the world's to God's by accepting discipline and correction. There is a benefit in going God's way. "But he who listens to me will live securely, And will be at ease from the dread of evil" (Proverbs 1:33).

Where wisdom is found

Wisdom is found in many places. Proverbs lists the gates, streets, top of the heights, and cross sections. Gates were the places of entrance in walled cities where older men would meet and discuss the news of the day. They would actually recite proverbs. They would sit or stand in a circle. The younger people would be outside of the circle but would listen to the older men discuss the daily news in the context of wisdom. Wisdom was found in the paths that led to the city center or marketplace. Here business was conducted. Wisdom was found and needed where decision-making happened, where relationships and interactions of business occurred. The heights were the towers. The lookouts needed to know how to recognize the friendly or the enemy approaching. Wisdom is found where people discern good from evil or the friendly person from the enemy. Proverbs is telling us that wisdom can be found in the real world where people are doing life.

But Proverbs says wisdom is not just found in places but with certain types of people. It only accompanies the humble, teachable, discerning, and the man of understanding. One of my favorite characters in the Bible is David. He had a lot of relationship problems. You could say his life was full of people drama. Yet God said that he was a man after His own heart. It was not because David was perfect.

Even a wise person sins and messes up. David was a man after God's own heart because he was teachable and humble. He learned to deal with things God's way.

David let various people speak into his life and was willing to be reproved and taught by them and God. For example, David was rebuked by the prophet Nathan when he took Bathsheba in adultery and had Uriah killed. He accepted the rebuke and correction. Another instance of David's wisdom is when David forsakes his anger and lets Abigail persuade him not to kill Nabal. Again, when his family and those of his men had been taken in 1 Samuel 24, David asked Abiathar, the priest, to call on God and ask Him what they should do. Further, when David had numbered the people, thereby sinning against God, he was truthful with himself. He confessed his sin and dealt with the consequences. He did not make excuses or lie to cover what he had done even when the whole nation knew they were dealing with consequences because their leader had sinned. In addition, David showed kindness to Saul's grandson, Mephibosheth, even in betrayal. Mephibosheth had stayed in Jerusalem when Absalom usurped the kingdom from David. Another instance was when David was older and went out to battle. He was almost killed. His mighty men told him he no longer should be in the thick of battle. David listened to his men's advice. In all these events, David feared God, knew himself, and admitted when he was wrong or needed help.

What wisdom teaches—character and relationships

Proverbs 3 gives us a list of eleven *do not* commands about what wisdom tells us to do.

Do not
- let kindness and truth leave you,
- lean on your own understanding,
- be wise in your own eyes,
- reject the discipline of the Lord,
- be afraid of sudden fear or the wicked,
- withhold good from those to whom it is due,
- refuse when a neighbor asks,

- devise harm against your neighbor,
- contend with a man without cause,
- envy a man of violence,
- choose the ways of a man of violence.

All these concern relationships. There is a skill in our relationship with God, our own character, and our relationship with others.

I love how Solomon instructs his son. He does not say be kind or be honest. He says, "Do not let kindness and truth leave you." These two things alone would make for good relationships. If we committed to using kindness and truth with every person we interacted with, relationships would be more fruitful and fulfilling. Can you imagine a marriage that used kindness and truth? Can you picture parents who used kindness and truth with their children? What would the work environment be like with kindness and truth present constantly? And, oh my, what would the government be like were kindness and truth bound each person's neck?

Kindness and truth are the keys to how we should treat others. The other relational commands all fall under this: *Do not refuse a neighbor's help* (kindness), *do not devise harm* (kindness), *do not contend with your neighbor* (kindness), and *do not envy* (kindness). This is why, in our home, one of our five rules is to be kind. We teach our children that kindness is attractive. People are drawn to someone who thinks and acts kindly toward others. Besides kindness, truth is the most important aspect of a good relationship. Truth will build trust. I am sure you know the story of the boy who cried wolf. The boy repeatedly says there is a wolf attacking the sheep, and the townspeople come out to protect the sheep. Each time, there is no wolf. The people lose trust in the boy because he lies. One day, a wolf really does come. He cries wolf, and no one comes to save the sheep because they do not believe him. Without truth, there is a lack of reliance and confidence. Picture your relationship as two people walking on a path. You are holding hands and doing life together. Kindness is what makes you want to walk with them. Truth is what holds you together as you walk on the same path. We cannot walk together and have companionship when one person lets go of the other. When one of my children tries to cover up their sin by lying, I lose trust in them. Our relationship is damaged. If wisdom is God's way and He says to not let kindness and truth leave, foolishness or Satan's way is unkindness and lies. The Bible says that Satan is the father of lies. The two first and foremost character qualities to teach your children are kindness and truth.

The next commands ("Do not lean on your own understanding" and "Do not be wise in your own eyes") concern our awareness of ourselves. Do we know who we are? Are we self-aware? God wants us to be aware of who we are and who we need. A life of wisdom leans on God for everything. A few years ago, I was sick. I had gone through some procedures and taken some medicine that had destroyed my digestive system. Somehow, my body had lost its ability to make stomach acid, so I literally could not digest food, and I could not fight off any bacteria without stomach acid. Without it, my stomach and intestine lining had no protection. I went through a period where I could hardly eat anything. I had to puree or juice most of my food. This led to a host of other problems. It took over a year to figure out the problem and then several other years to work on healing and restoration of my digestive system. During that time, the prayer of thanksgiving for my food became a literal "Bless this food to my body." I always thank God for my food, but during this time, it was a meal-by-meal plea that I would get some nutrients from the food I consumed. I needed God to help my body process food. This verse is telling us to plead to God for every situation, every decision, every choice in life, and every path we choose. Joshua was a good example of this. He prayed and asked God for wisdom over every enemy and city that the Israelites would attack. He consulted God for every decision and action as commander of the Lord's army.

The next two commands ("Do not reject the discipline of the Lord" and "Do not be afraid of sudden danger or the wicked") concern our relationship with God. The fear of the Lord is the beginning of wisdom. The fear of the Lord is to know who you are and who God is and to respond accordingly. If we fear God, we will accept His discipline because we know that He knows best. If we fear God, we will not fear the wicked, for we will know God is more powerful than they. When David brought the ark of the Lord to Jerusalem, he neglected to follow the instructions on how the ark was to be transported (by priests on poles). Instead, the Israelites brought the ark on a cart pulled by oxen. At one point, the ark was about to fall off the cart, and Uzzah touched it. He died instantly. David was upset with God, yet he realized how serious God was about His command. The next time he moved the ark, he did it according to God's specifications. When you do things wrong and receive consequences, are you able to receive and learn from them? The wise are humble and receive the discipline of the Lord.

The next six commands concern our relationship with others.

Do not
- withhold good from those to whom it is due,
- refuse when a neighbor asks,
- devise harm against your neighbor,
- contend with a man without cause,
- envy a man of violence,
- choose the ways of a man of violence.

These are all ideas we will see in Proverbs again. The wise is generous, a good friend and neighbor. The wise is not contentious nor evil toward his neighbor. He works to live at peace with others and avoids fighting and contention. The wise is self-controlled, not violent or angry. The wise person's heart is toward good.

Don't worry about all these details. Proverbs will teach us all about character and relationships.

Key to Relationships: Kindness and Truth

Personal Character	Relation to God	Relation to Others
Relies on God Aware of weaknesses and shortcomings Humble	Fears God, not man Accepts God's discipline Acknowledges God in all	Just Generous Not contentious Practices self-control Does not make evil or violent plans Good friend and neighbor

Concluding prayer

>Dear Lord,
>
>Help me to be teachable. Help me to lead as an example of someone who will turn to wisdom, listen to her, and be corrected when wrong. Help my children to have teachable hearts also. Let kindness and truth be apparent in our homes and in our interactions. Help these to be the keys we use in our relationships now and in the future. In Jesus's name, amen.
>
>Verse to pray: Proverbs 1:23

Practical Proverbs for the family

The naive
- Practice and act out kind and unkind acts: eyes, words, tone, body language.
- Read the stories of David and how he accepted the discipline of the Lord.
  - 2 Samuel 12:1–15
  - 1 Samuel 25:2–35

The youth and wise
- Read the sections of Proverbs on wisdom: What do you learn about wisdom? Where is she? What does she tell us to do? Underline the verbs. What benefits are there?
  - Proverbs 1:20–33
  - Proverbs 2:1–11
  - Proverbs 3:1–26, 27–35

Parent reflection and application

Use Proverbs's list as an evaluation: How are you doing in these areas?
Do not

- let kindness and truth leave you,
- lean on your own understanding,
- be wise in your own eyes,
- reject the discipline of the Lord,
- be afraid of sudden danger or the wicked,
- withhold good from those to whom it is due,
- refuse when a neighbor asks,
- devise harm against your neighbor,
- contend with a man without cause,
- envy a man of violence,
- choose the ways of a man of violence.

Reflect on one and pray about it.

CHAPTER 8

A Transcendent Pattern

> When I was a son to my father, tender and the only son in the sight of my mother, then he taught me and said to me…
>
> —Proverbs 4:3–4

Principle: The teachings of Proverbs should be ongoing from one generation to another. They are good for all time. There are whole life and body benefits to doing things God's way.

We've introduced wisdom, what it warns us of in chapter one, and what it looks like in chapter three. Now we will look at its rewards and benefits in chapter four and throughout the rest of the book.

All generations

Chapter 4 is interesting. Solomon is telling his son foundational things, but he stops to show him there is reason behind them. Picture him sitting in his beautiful gardens, reflecting and stopping for a moment to tell his son that this is God's pattern. He says this is something his father taught him when he was young. Even though we learned that Solomon asked God for wisdom, he gives some credit to David for passing on some of these things to him when he was young. "My father taught me too," he says. "It is not just me telling you. I had to learn it from my father, and you will have to tell your sons." That is the pattern and the job we are to do: continue God's truths from one generation to the next.

Psalm 78:4–7 says, "We will not conceal them from their children, But tell the generation to come the praises of the Lord, And His strength and His wondrous works that He has done. For He established a testimony in Jacob and appointed a law in Israel, which He commanded our fathers that they should teach them to their children, That the generation to come might know, even the children yet to be born, that they may arise and tell them to their children, That they should put their confidence in God and not forget the works of God, But keep His commandments."

Parents, we are stewards of God's truths, and part of our job is to pass those on to our children.

This perspective is important. Children may think that they are the only ones that have parents that tell them what to do. They don't see beyond themselves. We must help them see that what we teach, if it is from Scripture, transcends them, us, and our family. Truth lasts forever. It has worked in the past and will work in the future. Passing on truths is for their good but also for God's glory. It transcends one generation and one family. And it ultimately is not about us but about God.

A whole-body appeal

We have talked a lot about our responsibility. Here is the fun part: the rewards and benefits of wisdom. What will happen if we live a life of wisdom? Here is what Proverbs says:

Safety. "Do not forsake her, and she will guard you; Love her, and she will watch over you" (Proverbs 4:6).

In chapter 1, wisdom says that if you listen to her, you will live securely and be at ease from the dread of evil (1:33). We will not be afraid when we lie down, and our sleep will be sweet (3:24). We will be delivered and kept from the evil way, the perverse man, and the adulteress (2:12, 2:16, 7:5). Wisdom gives discernment and helps us beware, so when we avoid trouble whether it be a fight, uncontrolled anger, or violent men, we avoid the consequences of those actions and the unsafe situations they create. Therefore, a life of wisdom will protect us from evil. Wisdom helps lead us to safe places, people, and situations.

Honor/reputation. "Prize her, and she will exalt you; She will honor you if you embrace her. She will place on your head a garland of grace; She will present you with a crown of beauty" (Proverbs 4:8–9).

Wisdom gives us a good name and reputation because a person who is wise will do things well, whether using their craft, managing people, or dealing with problems. People are attracted to someone who does something well. That is the whole idea with professional athletes. People like to watch someone who is skillful at a sport. Being skillful at something makes your name known. *"Do you see a man skilled in his work? He will stand before kings; He will not stand before obscure men"* (Proverbs 22:29). The word "wisdom" was used in Exodus to describe the men who worked on the tabernacle furnishings. "Now the Lord spoke to Moses, saying, 'See, I have called by name Bezalel, the son of Uri, the son of Hur, of the tribe of Judah. I have filled him with the Spirit of God in wisdom, in understanding, in knowledge, and in all kinds of craftsmanship to make artistic designs for work in gold, in silver, and in bronze, and in the cutting of stones for settings, and in the carving of wood, that he may work in all kinds of craftsmanship'" (Exodus 31:1–5).

Health. "Hear, my son, and accept my sayings, and the years of your life will be many" (Proverbs 4:10).

A life of wisdom brings health benefits to our whole bodies. If we look back at Proverbs 3:7–8, it says, "Do not be wise in our own eyes; Fear the Lord and turn away from evil." And then it gives us the benefit: "It will be healing to your body and refreshment to your bones." A life of wisdom is good for our health. I've had my share of health problems. I actually had stage four endometriosis and, through that time, tried many of the traditional medical remedies to no avail. As I learned about natural remedies and health, I learned how food can be medicine. I changed my diet and began to eat less processed foods. The more closely what I put in my body resembled the original that God made, the better it was for me. God has created a way to health.

I have also struggled with anger. I hold it in and let it tear me apart from the inside. It has caused me physical problems such as lack of sleep and trouble digesting food. I found that when I forgive and deal with my anger problems, some of my health problems disappear. I sleep and eat better.

Strong footing/clear paths. "When you walk, your steps will not be impeded; And if you run, you will not stumble" (Proverbs 4:12).

Think of it this way. The more we walk in God's way, the fewer consequences of sin we must deal with. When we deal with the consequences of sin, we have stumbling blocks in our paths and added problems to life. Hebrews 12:1 says, "Therefore, since we have so great a cloud of witnesses surrounding us, let us also lay aside every encumbrance, and the sin which so easily entangles us, and let us run with endurance the race that is set before us." Did you catch what that verse says about sin? It entangles and encumbers us. It weighs us down. It is like running a race and carrying a duffel bag on your shoulders. Aren't you more likely to stumble and fall when carrying a heavy load? A life of wisdom helps us to experience what Jesus said: "My yoke is easy, and my burden is light" (Matthew 11:30). We need to teach our children that when we walk with wisdom, we will avoid the consequences and pain of sin. It doesn't mean life will be easy, but wisdom saves us from the heartache and pain that naturally comes with sin.

Discernment. "Then you will discern the fear of the Lord and discover the knowledge of God. Then you will discern righteousness, justice, equity, and every good course" (Proverbs 2:5, 9). Discernment is the ability to judge and make good decisions. This is the wisdom that Solomon asked for in 1 Kings 3: the ability to judge and discern between good and evil. Wisdom gives us this important skill. Good decisions lead to many benefits. Think of the important decisions one makes in life: who to marry, where to live, which career path to pursue, how to spend money, how to vote, and so on. Do you see how wisdom's profit is better than silver and its gain is better than gold? Wisdom's benefits are the consequences of good decisions.

Life. "Watch over your heart with all diligence, for from it flow the springs of life" (Proverbs 4:23). Deuteronomy 6:5 says, "You shall love the Lord your God with all your heart, with all your soul, and with all your might." The word for "heart" is the same one used in Proverbs to mean the inner man. It is strictly opposite to the outer man. It is not talking about the heart as the seat of emotions but the whole inner person—all that makes a person who they are, separate from their body or physical part. This means Solomon is speaking about the mind, will, and emotions of a person. Every thought, desire, emotion, and behavior comes from this inner place that we are to rule with wisdom. Solomon is pleading with his son to let wisdom be his main counselor and adviser to his inner person as if this inner person is the president who will make decisions from the Oval Office, and wisdom is the adviser. He is to guard that command center.

Concluding prayer

> Dear Lord,
>
> Wisdom has many benefits. You are so good to us for wanting us to have all these blessings. Help me to acquire wisdom, to prize her, and to call her a friend so that I may have the benefits of a life lived in God's way. Help me to pass on wisdom's ways to future generations. In Jesus's name, amen.
>
> Verse to pray: Proverbs 4:6

Practical Proverbs for the family

The naive
- Read about Solomon's wisdom again. List the good things he had because of wisdom (1 Kings 10:1–9).

The youth and wise
- Read the sections of Proverbs on wisdom and look for the benefits of walking in wisdom.

    - Proverbs 1:20–33
    - Proverbs 2:1–11
    - Proverbs 3:1–26, 27–35
    - Proverbs 4:1–27

Parent reflection and application

Stop and reflect on the different areas of life: spiritual, vocational, relational, educational, recreational, and physical. How can wisdom help you? What benefits will wisdom bring you?

Safety	Honor/ Reputation	Health	Strong Footing/ Clear Path	Discernment	Life

CHAPTER 9

Wisdom: The Person and the Relationship

Does not wisdom call?

—Proverbs 9:1a

Wisdom has built her house.

—Proverbs 8:1a

Principle: We need a growing relationship with wisdom.

Proverbs 8–9 gives us a personification of wisdom. These are the final treatises on wisdom. This section is the end of the foundation training stage. Chapter 8 tells us the characteristics of wisdom. Chapter 9 gives us the invitation of the woman of wisdom and the woman of folly. It will show us that there are two paths we can take. We must choose which invitation to accept.

The wisdom of God

Proverbs 8 personifies wisdom. It tells how wisdom was with God at creation. They both are there working together and taking pleasure in God's work. Proverbs 8:30–31a says, "Then I was beside Him, as a master workman; And I was daily His delight, Rejoicing always before Him, Rejoicing in the world, His earth." The meaning of "rejoice" in this verse is "to laugh." Picture God commanding creation into existence. Wisdom is laughing at the beauty and artistry of God's work. They are working together and having fun.

There are two things we can take away from this image of wisdom. First, we are to have a relationship with her as God does. At the beginning of the chapter, wisdom calls out to men. She wants them to listen to her, to dwell with her, and to utilize her. She says, "By me kings reign and rulers decree justice." She is inviting us to have a relationship with her. She wants to be our friend.

What do you do with a friend? You spend time with her. You have fun together. You laugh together. You talk and listen to each other. You know each other's likes and needs. You can buy friends gifts for their birthday without having to ask them what they want. You might even know what your friend would think or say in a certain situation. You help each other when in need or discouraged. Wisdom wants to do those things with us. We should spend time with her, know her, and know what she would want in a certain situation. We should laugh with her. When we see God do something in someone's life, we should rejoice at the wonder of Him. We should call her a friend.

The second thing noticeable about this chapter is the character traits of wisdom and her part in creation. She resembles the person of Jesus Christ. First Corinthians 1:24 says that Jesus Christ is the wisdom of God. Proverbs 8:12–14 lists seven things that wisdom dwells with: prudence, knowledge, discretion, fear of the Lord, counsel, understanding, and power. Two other places in Scripture speak of the seven attributes of wisdom. The first is Isaiah 11:1–5, which is a passage speaking about the Messiah, saying that He is the Spirit of the Lord and has the Spirit of wisdom, understanding, counsel, strength, knowledge, fear of the Lord, and justice. Again, here, there are seven descriptions of the Messiah's Spirit. James 3:17 also speaks on the wisdom from above and includes a list of seven attributes: pure, peaceable, gentle, reasonable, full of mercy and good fruits, unwavering, and without hypocrisy. The chart below lists the three passages and the attributes listed in each. Revelation 4:5 says there are seven lampstands that represent the seven spirits of God. These also could be the complete characteristics of the Holy Spirit who rested on Jesus. The principle here is that Jesus Christ is the wisdom of God. He is the ultimate example of wisdom, a life lived skillfully for God. These characteristics were ultimately and perfectly displayed in Jesus Christ, who was filled with the Holy Spirit. If we want to live life skillfully and godly, we must have a relationship with the One who displayed wisdom perfectly and be filled with His Holy, complete Spirit.

7 Pillars of Wisdom (Cross-references)

Proverbs 8:12–14	Isaiah 11:1–5	James 3:17
Wisdom dwells with…	The Spirit of the Lord…the spirit of…	Wisdom from above is…
Prudence	Wisdom	Pure
Knowledge	Understanding	Peaceable
Discretion	Counsel	Gentle
Fear of the Lord	Strength	Reasonable
Counsel	Knowledge	Full of mercy and good fruits
Understanding	Fear of the Lord	Unwavering
Power	Justice	Without hypocrisy

A relationship with wisdom

Let's get back to the idea of a relationship with wisdom. Proverbs gives us this idea of a growing relationship with wisdom. Wisdom should be something we grow in just as a relationship grows. Think about when you first meet someone. Being in the homeschool ministry, I get to meet a lot of people. The first time I meet someone, it is usually through email or a phone call. They hear of our ministry or find us online, and they make an inquiry. Usually, the person tells me about themselves and their children, and then they tell me their needs or what they are looking for. Then we progress to meeting in person, and if the relationship continues, they participate in our programs. One friend I met this way contacted me because she was going to homeschool her sons. I remember talking to her on the phone in my backyard. As we got to know each other, we realized we had a lot in common and got along well. Our boys liked each other and looked forward to being with each other. Now our friendship has evolved to the point that we see each other regularly. We reach out to each other when one of us needs prayer or help. We share needs and ideas with each other. One day, I had my fingernails painted. She was surprised because she knew that I was not a girly person. I work in my yard and garden too much to have nice nails. My behavior was not in the norm that she knew. We know what positions, roles, and activities the other would like. We can even predict what the other might be thinking because we have gotten to know each other so well.

But friendships can dissolve or fall apart. You just don't keep up with each other. You lose something in common. One changes or grows, and the other one doesn't. It is like this with wisdom. It is a relationship that can either grow or dissolve. We first listen and get to know her. We discover what kinds of things she likes and what she does. We learn what she is good at. Then we value her. We like her so much that we set aside time for her, and we prioritize seeing her regularly, as we do with our friends. We will find time in our busy schedule. We seek wisdom out and make sure we check in with her and find her. When we get wisdom, we know her responses to situations. As we know what our friend would want, we know what wisdom would want because we have her as a friend. We must make sure we continue to walk with her, or our relationship with her will dissolve.

The image below will help you see the growing relationship with wisdom. The verbs in bold are the ones Proverbs uses to describe the relationship with wisdom. The verbs that are not bold are ways you can accomplish those commands. As you can see in the image below, it grows on a scale, with listening being the first step to being intimate with her.

Our growing relationship with wisdom

Listen, pay attention, incline ear/heed instruction	Prize, love	Search, seek, find	Acquire, get, take	Do not forsake, keep	Call it intimate
Heed instruction from God, His Word, wise people, and authorities in your life. Read about wise people in the past (Hebrews 11), and read good books.	Prioritize wise things and people with your time and money.	Wisdom is found in the humble, teachable, and discerning. Identify those people and seek to spend time with them. Wisdom is not found with the scoffer, fool, or selfish. Avoid these.	Take possession of wisdom. Own it by making it part of you. Fill yourself with it, practice it, and recognize it. The rod and reproof give wisdom. Be teachable and correctable. Pray for it / Lord gives it (James 1:7).	Memorize verses and sayings about wisdom. Review them by rereading Proverbs. Do it often. Practice wisdom. You don't want to forget her.	Be close to wise people. Have a mentor. Keep company with wiser people.

What does this scale look like in life?

As the skill of listening grows, so does our relationship with wisdom. As parents, we must facilitate our children in this growing relationship.

We have already talked about the first step to getting wisdom, and that is to listen. (See chapter 4.)

Prize wisdom. Our children will see what we value by seeing what we spend our time and money on. Prize wisdom by prioritizing your time and money on wise things, books, and people.

Seek and search. One thing I regularly do is seek out people who are smarter than me. I love being around people that make me better. This is a form of seeking wisdom. A regular prayer in our home is that we would be wise and godly friends and that we would find godly and wise friends. Ask someone over for dinner whom you admire. Seek a mentor.

Acquire or get wisdom. One prayer God will always answer yes to is the prayer for wisdom, "but if any of you lacks wisdom, let him ask of God, who gives to all men generously and without reproach, and it will be given to him" (James 1:5). Proverbs says that the rod and reproof give wisdom. The best way to get wisdom is to be teachable and humble enough to be corrected. Be a learner. Read good books. Read about wise people such as leaders, missionaries, and hymn writers. Get it by acquiring a bank of good examples you can imitate.

Do not forsake it. Keep it. Have you ever lost knowledge, a memory, or even the ability to be in shape? When we don't practice something, we lose it. Wisdom needs to be practiced and not forgotten. We need to review it and memorize it. Come back to her often.

Wisdom and folly's invitation

A few years ago, we moved to an area of town that had more land and was near to the Rio Grande. We wanted a more rural and outdoor lifestyle where our five boys could enjoy more outdoor space. We could have gardens and animals and have nature be more accessible. We moved out of our old house, and the renters were contracted to be in by a certain date. Well, the people we were buying the house from asked for more time to move out, so we were caught without a place to live for two weeks.

Graciously, one family in our church invited all seven of us to move into their home! My friend is such a hospitable person. She had a gift basket in the room with snacks and little items to make me feel welcome. They gave us a whole wing to their home, shared meals with us, and never made us feel uncomfortable or unwanted.

Proverbs 9 is one of my favorites. Wisdom and folly are hostesses. They are both personified as women who prepare their homes and a table to invite men to join them. The two are to be compared, and the question begs, which home do you want to go to? Let's look at each.

Wisdom builds her own house and hews out seven pillars. She chops down and shapes the pillars for her home. She has methodically prepared to invite you to her home. She then slaughters an animal and mixes wine to serve her guests. She sets her table and sends out her maidens to call in guests. Specifically, she invites the naive and him who lack understanding.

I love homemade food, and I am not the best cook. When I had my last son, someone from our church made us homemade fried chicken! It was so good. Here, wisdom is preparing things from scratch. She wants it to be good. She cares enough to prioritize her time to do this for others. She is thoughtful and methodical. Wisdom wants to give her guests good sustenance and sound structure in their lives. Wisdom's guests will have a life that is built well and endures.

In contrast, the woman of folly is not noted to have built anything. She steals food to serve her guests, and they must eat it secretly. The woman of folly sits at her doorway and the high places in the city to cry out to those who pass by. She spends more time and effort to invite people than to prepare. Her meal does not last or give sustenance. She wants the simple-minded and naive, the one who lacks understanding. Folly's invitation is to anyone she can catch and bring in. She leads her guests to death. The woman of folly's purpose is to have temporary delight and pleasure.

Concluding prayer

> Dear Lord,
>
> Thank You for being so clear with us and showing us that there are only two ways or paths to follow in life. Help me to choose wisdom's way. Give me discernment so I can tell the difference. Help me to teach my kids the difference between the two. Please work in their hearts, that they may choose wisdom's way also. If we get off the path, please bring others, Your Word, and Your Spirit to cause us to return quickly. In Jesus's name, amen.
>
> Verse to pray: 1 Kings 3:9

Practical Proverbs for the family

The naive
- Talk about a best friend. What makes you like them? What do you do together? Extend the idea to that of a friendship with wisdom.
- Read the story of David and Jonathan in 1 Samuel 18:1–5

The youth
- Read the sections of Proverbs on wisdom.
- Proverbs 8–9 compare wisdom and folly and give examples of each. Use the chart as a guide.

Wisdom	Folly

The wise
- List examples of how you would live out these commands about wisdom. How would you practically do these verbs to build a relationship with wisdom?

Listen, pay attention, incline ear, heed	
Prize, love	
Search, seek, find	
Acquire, get, take	
Do not forsake, keep	
Call it your friend	

Parent reflection and application

Think of wisdom as a guest that you invite into your home. What can you do to make her welcome? How can you exercise wisdom?

SECTION 2: GROWING INDEPENDENCE

Building Character in the Youth— The Conversation Stage

In Proverbs 10:1, Solomon reintroduces himself, "The proverbs of Solomon. A wise son makes a father glad, But a foolish son is grief to his mother." This section begins the longest section of Proverbs, where one of the main themes is the comparison of the two ways of life: God's way and man's way. Other words he uses for this comparison are the wise versus the foolish and the righteous versus the wicked. The method he uses to teach this concept is comparison through examples, images, and natural consequences of the two ways. We will see in chapter 16 that the motivation for being wise ultimately is God Himself. Solomon will bring out three categories of each way: character, relationships, and responsibility.

I call this the conversation stage because the main means parents use during these years—the bulk of childhood—is talk. There is some training. But instruction is done through conversation. Solomon talks to his son. He tells him stories. He gives descriptions.

Chapter 12 is the first time Solomon mentions the word "man" in the context of describing how his son should behave. He has moved from the first stage of rearing, where he appeals to his son using the words "My son." Now he describes a "man of…" to explain to his son the two types of men he can become.

CHAPTER 10

A Comparison of Two Ways

> The way of a fool is right in his own eyes, But a
> wise man is he who listens to counsel.
>
> —Proverbs 12:15

Principle: There are two ways of life—God's (the wise) and man's (the foolish). There is a progression of wisdom and a progression of foolishness. Comparing these two ways helps us to grow in discernment.

Comparison of the two men / two ways of life

Proverbs 10 through 15 contain a list of contrasts. Just skim through the chapters. You will see the word "but" a lot. What is he doing? He is comparing two ways of life. He is teaching his son the two ways you can go in life based on the two invitations we just saw. He is listing the characteristics of a wicked or foolish person versus those of a righteous or wise person. Simple, right? Jesus did this in the Sermon on the Mount. He told the people about the expectations for His kingdom. He said things like, "This is what you have heard in the past, but this is what I tell you to do now." He compared the new to the old. Then he gave them a list of parables starting with the phrase "The kingdom of God is like…" He was giving images of what God's kingdom was like versus that of man's. Solomon does the same thing.

This is the stage where we will work on character and habits with our child. The main method we use is comparison. The main tool is conversation. This stage involves a lot of talking with your child, even when they mess up. Remember 1 Timothy 3:16 and the four verbs we do as parents—teach, reprove, correct, and train? Talk to them about the right way. Reprove or warn them of the wrong way. Correct them when they get off the right way, and punish them if necessary. Then train them. Have them practice the right way.

It is important that we put some responsibility on them. They must choose the right or wrong way. Parents, we must give them some freedom to make choices. They will make bad ones. But while they are with us, they have the cushion of our help when they fall and mess up.

Since we will be talking about the wise and foolish, let's make sure we have the right definitions and understand what wisdom and foolishness are.

Wisdom, understanding, and knowledge

There are three key words in Proverbs: knowledge, understanding, and wisdom. There is a progression in the three as we have seen a progression in three types of people (naive, youth, and wise). There is a progression in the content also.

When children are young, they are excited and want to tell you or show you what they are learning about. This is the knowledge stage. Knowledge is the facts or information, the things we memorize. We acquire knowledge by experience or a relationship. The implication of the Hebrew word for knowledge is that knowledge is usually the result of others. This makes sense in the light of knowledge being the foundation. One who is more knowledgeable teaches the one who is less knowledgeable. Gaining knowledge doesn't end. We build on it and get deeper.

Understanding concerns the next level, the heart. The word for "heart" in the Bible can be translated as either heart or mind. It is the core of the being, the inner person. Understanding takes knowledge and moves beyond just repeating it. It talks about it, explains it, asks questions, wrestles with it, or expresses it in some form. Understanding is knowing what it means. Understanding helps us to wrap our being around something. In the Bible, understanding also has a moral connotation. God desires both a cognitive and moral understanding of truth. He desires that the facts penetrate the mind and then lead the heart to feel and act upon the facts. God never intended for knowledge to be the goal. He does not want heads full of knowledge that do nothing but spout out information.

Wisdom is the third level. It is the skill to apply it. Wisdom can use knowledge and understanding in a different situation than the one in which it was learned. Wisdom is using knowledge, the mind's understanding, and the heart's emotions to act in a way that would honor God. The word in Hebrew for wisdom implies experience or shrewdness. In the Bible, wisdom is used to describe men and women who were skillful in physical tasks such as building the tabernacle and its furnishings (see Exodus 35: 25–26, 31). It describes skillfulness in social abilities as when Joseph interpreted dreams (Genesis 41:14–36).

Knowledge	Understanding	Wisdom
(The Information)	(The Moral Conscience)	(The Act/Skill)
Learning, insight, notion (about half of the times mentioned in Proverbs). It can be memorized.	Comprehension with strong moral connotations, inner man including mind, will, and emotions. It can be explained.	Skill, experience, shrewdness, the living out. It can be used in different situations.

Fool, fool, and scoffer

There are two words in Hebrew that are translated as "fool" in English. The first is *kesil,* which means stupid or dull. A good picture of what it means is thick. It communicates the idea of not wanting to grow, learn, or receive instruction. This person is not teachable. You can't converse with them. They will just argue with you. They are unreliable and repeat mistakes. They are like a dog that returns to his vomit (Proverbs 26:11). They bring sorrow to their parents.

The second word for "fool" is evil, and it means perverse or morally bad. These people progress to a foolishness that is morally wrong. They despise wisdom. They know the right thing to do and choose not to do it. They want to do evil. They like fighting. They tear down relationships. They reject discipline or correction. Unlike the first fool, who is unteachable, this fool knows the right way and refuses to choose it.

Proverbs adds the word *scoffer* to this list of those who are opposed to God's ways and wisdom. The scoffer reaches the highest level of foolishness and wickedness by mocking good. In his heart, he feels scorn. He expresses that emotion outwardly. Not only does he do evil, but he mocks those that do good. As Proverbs mentions a three-part progression to wisdom, it also mentions this three-part progression to foolishness.

The Fool	The Fool	The Scoffer
(The Stupid)	(The Morally Bad)	(The Mocker)
Doesn't want to learn. Unteachable.	Chooses to do wrong. It is like a sport to him.	Makes fun of good. Has bitterness toward those who do right.

As wisdom has natural benefits, foolishness has natural consequences. The fool brings grief, destruction, waste, and pain through conflict. Proverbs gives us two commands regarding fools. First, *do not get into an argument with them*. Sometimes, it is better to just walk away. It also warns us *not to hire a fool*, for they waste and destroy. Literally, they swallow oil and treasure.

More importantly, we are not to be fools. We are to beware ourselves and warn our children of the undesirable lifestyle of a fool. We do not want to be people who destroy, display dishonor, bring grief to others, waste resources, refuse to learn, are arrogant, cause fights, and lose our tempers. One exercise you can do with your kids is to look at the verses in this section. List what it says about the fool and discuss what the life of a fool would look like. Is it appealing? Is it a lifestyle worth pursuing?

With younger children, we can teach about foolishness when they do not want to learn or listen to instructions. We can tell them that when they refuse to listen and learn, they are acting like a fool. The path of a fool is not good. It is like a dog who returns to his vomit (Proverbs 26:11). That visual got the attention of my young boys!

One of my favorite verses to pray for my kids is Psalm 1. It says, "How blessed is the man who does not walk in the counsel of the wicked, nor stand in the path of sinners, nor sit in the seat of scoffers! But his delight is in the law of the Lord, and in His law he meditates day and night, and he will be like a tree firmly planted by streams of water, which yields its fruit in season, and its leaf does not wither; and in whatever he does, he prospers." I think it is interesting that Psalm 1 has a similar three-part progression of evil influence: the wicked, the sinners, and the scoffers. Look at the progression of behavior. First, he walks with them, then he stands with them, and finally, he sits with them. Each time, the man gets more comfortable with evil.

Now that we hopefully understand the foolish and wise ways and the levels of progression, we can look at the two ways of life and see that we can grow in each. What does each look like, and how do we become fools or wise?

When I studied these lists, I noticed that they compared the two ways in three areas: personal character, personal responsibility, and relational skills. Parents, you are building the second tier of the foundation. Think of it as three areas: the inner self (character), the outer self (relational), and the part that stewards God's creation (responsibility). The table below shows some of the main differences between the wise and the fool, the righteous and the wicked.

The righteous/wise	*Fool/wicked*
Wise character—self	Foolish character
Wise relationships—people	Foolish relationships
Wise stewardship—responsibilities	Foolish stewardship
Diligent	Negligent
Teachable	Unteachable
Full of integrity	Deceptive
Loving	Hateful
Discerning	Impulsive
Uses self-control	Lacks control
Productive	Lazy
Has a hard work ethic	Cheater
Just	Proud
Humble	Tears down
Edifying	Critical
Encouraging	Untrustworthy
Trustworthy	Cruel
Merciful	Perverse
Blameless	Gossip
Discrete	Selfish
Generous	Undisciplined
Disciplined	Self-centered
Insightful	Cruel
Compassionate	Foolish
Prudent	Wavering
Firmly established	Arrogant
Esteemed	

Let's break each category down and look at some qualities in each.

1. *Character.* In the first section, we talked about building upon the foundation of kindness and truth. Do not let kindness and truth leave you; bind them around your neck, write them on the tablet of your heart (Proverbs 3:3).

You've established that godly character is built on a heart of kindness and truth.

The next things we add to character are teachability, integrity/honesty, trustworthiness, and self-control.

Receives instruction

Teachability is one of the first differences we learn between the wise and the fool. The wise are *teachable*; the fool will refuse to learn. The wise will receive instruction and listen to reproof and correction. The wise want to grow and improve. A fool is wise in his own eyes. He is arrogant and thinks he knows it all. He will not listen nor receive instructions. This is why the first step to being wise is being teachable.

How do we teach teachability? It starts with us. We must set examples of teachability first and foremost by being in God's Word and letting our kids know that we are learning from God's Word. Share with your kids what you are learning. Our family does this at dinnertime. One of our conversational questions is "What have you learned today?" We are pretty open with our children. We share with them plans, ideas, problems, and failures. We are a little bit like our own support group. I ask my kids regularly to pray for me and give them my prayer requests. I still am the authority, but I want them to see that Tim and I are human. We are weak and wrong at times. We need to be teachable.

The last year and a half has been one of many transitions in our home. One day, we were all on each other. Everyone was impatient. We had been fighting a lot. I was yelling. The boys were constantly at odds. I decided that we would start the day with some reflection. I had them all get in the car and told them to be quiet the whole drive. We would go somewhere to talk and try to reset our relationships a little. I asked them each to think of something they did that was causing relationships in our home to be broken or strained. Then I wanted them to pray. We headed to Barnes and Noble. As we went, I thought of myself but also all the things I could tell them they were doing wrong. We got out and got ourselves a treat from the bakery as well as some coffee for me. We sat down, and I read them Hebrews 12:1. I told them, "We are running a race. This life is our race, and sin weighs us down. If you were running a race, what would you carry with you? Do you want to carry a bag of soil or an oven on your back?" Then I asked them to name a sin they needed to get rid of. They each shared things. "Being quick to get angry at my brothers." "Arguing before obeying." The Holy Spirit had convicted them of their sin. We confessed to one another and suggested verses to help us. We prayed and then had some fun. My point in this story is that, as parents, we must guide our children in being taught by the Holy Spirit. The Holy Spirit is our teacher and guides us into truth. Here are some verses for you to pray and meditate on about being teachable.

- Listen to counsel and accept discipline, that you may be wise the rest of your days (Proverbs 19:20).
- The wise of heart will receive commands, but a babbling fool will be ruined (Proverbs 10:8).
- For the commandment is a lamp and the teaching is light; and reproofs for discipline are the way of life (Proverbs 6:23).

Integrity

Another important characteristic is *integrity*. This is the next step, built on truth and kindness toward others. In a way, it combines the two.

The word integrity comes from a verb that means to be complete. Look at this definition from Noah Webster's 1828 Dictionary: "The entire, unimpaired state of any thing, particularly of the mind; moral soundness or purity; incorruptness; uprightness; honesty. *Integrity* comprehends the whole moral character but has a special reference to uprightness in mutual dealings, transfers of property, and agencies for others."

A person of integrity makes decisions based on moral principles, not emotional whims, cultural trends, traditions, worldly ideas, or philosophies. Integrity means using principles of truth to guide you. A person of wisdom or righteousness is guided not by "We've done it this way" reasoning. He questions everything: "Does this align with Scripture?" "What does God say?"

I heard a lady tell the story of how she became a believer. She was a relativist, believed everyone could make up their own rules or truth in life, and there was nothing constant. She was telling me about her favorite book, *Jane Eyre*. She told me that the book made her see the value and necessity of absolutes. The main character in the book, Jane Eyre, falls in love with her employer, Edward Rochester. On her wedding day, she discovers Rochester is still married. Rochester pleads with Jane to run away to France, where they can marry. Jane refuses to marry him on moral principles. The lady who spoke explained that the book helped her understand that when storms come in life, you need principles to live by. You can't make up the rules with each new storm. You need to know the rules and principles you will live by before the storms and circumstances in life come. Integrity gives us a rule book so that when life happens, we know what play to make.

Here are some images Proverbs gives us for integrity and trustworthiness. Choose some of your favorite ones, memorize them, and use them to remind your family of the characteristics of the wise.

- The integrity of the upright will guide them, but the crookedness of the treacherous will destroy them (Proverbs 11:3).
- A good name is to be more desired than great wealth, favor is better than silver and gold (Proverbs 22:1).

Integrity causes the wise to be firmly established while, in contrast, the fool is wavering. This is not a characteristic we think of much, but the idea is to be strong in our beliefs to stand when the storm comes. Proverbs 24:3 says that understanding will establish our home. It will make it firm. When troubles and attacks come, we will be able to stand. The fool and the wicked waver and stumble because they are established in their own ways.

Imagine the earth. Looking at it from space, you see the green land, the blue water, and the white clouds. On top of that earth is you. You stand as the owner and the ultimate authority. That is what a fool does. He makes the way and the rules. He is the authority on everything. He is the maker of his own truth. He is not submitted to a higher authority. Psalm 14:1 states, "The fool says in his heart there is no god." A fool makes *himself* god, a dangerous place to be.

Self-control

This one is important! Self-control builds on the foundational idea of beware. But we must not just beware of others that may lead us astray but of ourselves and our own temptations and weaknesses. The character of a wise person can control or manage their thoughts, emotions, and behavior. They are self-aware and on guard to the things that will destroy them from the inside out that will damage their character, relationships, and responsibilities. Self-control is simply self-government.

To help your kids with self-control, you must help them to know themselves. Where are they vulnerable? Do they seek physical pleasure? Do they spout out the first thing that comes to their mind? Do they have a temper? Help them to see their weaknesses. Ask God to help them be on guard to those. Ask the Holy Spirit to help them manage themselves. Self-control is so valuable that Solomon speaks about it in the next section in light of anger, the tongue, wine, and women. We will look at each of these in the next chapters.

2. *Relational.* The wise will relate to people with generosity, compassion, trust, and justice. Now we are building on the list of do nots from chapter three. The wise person sees the needs of others and meets them. They build others up. They invest in relationships with others by being reliable and trustworthy. Yet the fool is unkind and selfish. He will speak words that bring death and discouragement. He holds back from the poor and tears relationships down. Proverbs

14:1 summarizes this: "The wise woman builds her house, but the foolish tears it down with her own hands."

Generosity

All that we have is given by God, and we are His stewards. A wise person realizes who really owns it all and can, therefore, be generous to others, knowing that God is the provider and giver of all things. When something needs to be picked up or cleaned in our house, we don't necessarily ask our kids to do it according to what is theirs or who made the mess. We tell them it is all God's—our home, toys, food, animals, books, etc. They have personal responsibilities, but when something needs to be done, we ask them to take care of it because it is God's. We take care of the toy that brother got out, the animal that needs to be fed, the groceries that need to be put away, or the floor that needs to be vacuumed because they are all things God has given us. When we have the idea that it is not ours but God's, it is easier to share.

One who is gracious to a poor man lends to the Lord, and He will repay him for his good deed (Proverbs 19:17).

The generous man will be prosperous, and he who waters will himself be watered (Proverbs 11:25).

Compassion

Compassion is an awareness of others at the emotional level. A compassionate person has an awareness of other people to the point that they can feel for them whether or not they have experienced the same thing. This requires less focus on the self.

One day, I hurt my back. I was in so much pain I was throwing up. I could hear one of my sons crying through the door as he sat in the hallway next to the bathroom, worrying about me. A wise person is compassionate for the same reason that they are generous. They know that God is the creator of people and animals and will treat them as such. Both compassion and generosity build on the kindness we tie around our necks (Proverbs 3:3).

A righteous man has regard for the life of his animal, but even the compassion of the wicked is cruel (Proverbs 12:10).

Trustworthiness

Trustworthiness, like integrity, lets others know that you will base your decisions and behavior on principle, not whims. A principled person is reliable because their character and behavior are predictable. In addition, because a wise person has self-control, others can trust he will manage reactions and emotions. Trustworthiness builds on truth from the first section. When we live by truth, we establish principles we can live by in any situation. When we relate in truth, we are trustworthy, for our word is reliable. Notice the great visuals in this verse:

He who goes about as a talebearer reveals secrets, But he who is trustworthy conceals a matter (Proverbs 11:13).

3. *Responsibility*
    Production/work ethic
    Another difference between the wise and foolish is their work ethic and the way they attain wealth. The wise person is a diligent and disciplined worker. He is reliable to his master. The fool, on the other hand, is lazy. He will make excuses not to work: "There is a lion outside in the square." He expects easy wealth, and he earns wages deceptively. Wealth should not be earned by ruthlessness, treachery, stealing, or fraud. The fool cheats people. One phrase my father-in-law says is "You have to grow with your money." There are plenty of cases of young people who came into a lot of money and did not handle it well. According to Solomon, enduring wealth is gained in an honest way, shared with others, and passed down to future generations. The pictures in this section are hilarious. These are great to share with your kids and help them see a fun picture of these important truths. Try acting them out.

- Like vinegar to the teeth and smoke to the eyes, so is the lazy one to those who send him (Proverbs 10:26).
- The sluggard buries his hand in the dish, but will not even bring it back to his mouth (Proverbs 19:24).
- He also who is slack in his work Is brother to him who destroys (Proverbs 18:9).
- Do not weary yourself to gain wealth, cease from your consideration of it. When you set your eyes on it, it is gone. For wealth certainly makes itself wings Like an eagle that flies toward the heavens (Proverbs 23:4–5).

Justice

I did not realize how much God cares about justice. He does not like it when the weak, helpless, and innocent are taken advantage of, especially by those in power. As we grow and mature, God requires us to care more for justice. It is a responsibility the wise person is tasked with. Justice extends kindness and integrity, for it treats others based on principle and law, which should be based on truth. Noah Webster's 1828 Dictionary's definition of justice is "The virtue which consists in giving to everyone what is his due; practical conformity to the laws and to principles of rectitude in the dealings of men with each other; honesty; integrity in commerce or mutual intercourse." Part of Solomon's purpose in writing Proverbs as stated in chapter one was to "receive instruction in wisdom, justice, and equity." It isn't really something I thought of before, teaching my kids justice, yet God says it is more important to Him than sacrifice. Micah 6:8 says, "He has told you, O man, what is good; And what does the LORD require of you But to do justice, to love kindness, And to walk humbly with your God?"

Following are more examples of justice in this section of Proverbs. Again, choose some of your favorite ones, memorize them, and use them to remind your family of the characteristics of the wise.

- By me (wisdom) kings reign, and rulers decree justice (Proverbs 8:15).

- A false balance is an abomination to the Lord, but a just weight is His delight (Proverbs 11:1).
- To do righteousness and justice Is desired by the Lord more than sacrifice (Proverbs 21:3).

Character—Inner Self	Relationships—Outward	Responsibility—Steward
Teachable Full of integrity Discerning Self-controlled Humble Blameless Discreet Disciplined Insightful Prudent Firmly established	Compassionate Encouraging Loving Just Edifying Esteemed Merciful Trustworthy	Diligent Productive Hardworking Generous Disciplined Trustworthy Just

Concluding prayer

Dear Lord,

Help me to discern between foolish and wise behavior. Help me to grow in wise character. Give me the wisdom to understand these and teach my kids by example. Help our family to be people who are teachable, humble, and of integrity. May we examine ourselves and see our weaknesses and areas of temptation while gaining self-control over them. Help us to look at our resources as Yours and be productive with what You have given us. Then help us to be generous. May we be good, hard-working, reliable stewards of all You've given. Help us to look at others and be compassionate. May we love truth and justice and treat others based on principle. Dear Lord, help us to have wise character, wise relationships, and wise stewardship. We love You for guiding and helping us. In Jesus's name, amen.

Verse to pray: Psalm 90:12

Practical Proverbs for the family

The naive
- Make sure your young child knows that the first step to being wise is to be teachable. Emphasize the importance of learning, listening, and fearing God. Memorize Proverbs 1:7, "The fear of the Lord is the beginning of knowledge; fools despise wisdom and instruction."

The youth and wise
- Read Proverbs 10–15 and make a list contrasting the wise and the foolish and the wicked and the good. Discuss it together.

The Wise	The Foolish

Parent reflection

Use the chart to reflect on wise character, relationships, and responsibility. What characteristics of each could you grow in? Choose one verse in each to pray on and ask God to help you with.

Wise Character	Wise Relationships	Wise Responsibility

CHAPTER 11

The Sovereignty of God—
A Second Appeal to God

Commit your works to the Lord and your plans will be established.

—Proverbs 16:3

Principle: God's way is best and brings benefits. He is the motivation to do the right thing.

Our view of God determines our view of people, ourselves, work, stewardship, and possessions. This chapter gives us the motivation to follow the right way. We are to do the right thing because God desires us to. He is worthy to be obeyed because of His great character. It is as if Solomon is saying, "You know what, son? God is going to have His way. He knows best. Why wouldn't you just submit to Him? I have shown you the two ways and their results. Just follow Him!" Here is what Solomon says about God.

The eyes of the Lord are everywhere, watching the evil and the good (15:3). God sees all. This is why the rules we teach should be God's, not ours. We should do the right thing when our parents are not around and when our teachers are not watching because God sees all. Nothing is hidden from Him, and ultimately, our children will answer to God, not us.

Teach your kids: God is omnipresent—everywhere.

The plans of the heart belong to man, But the answer of the tongue is from the Lord (16:1). God gives us the ability to express what is in our hearts through our words. Our breath, and therefore our ability to speak, is from Him. The prophets each spoke what God instructed them to. God even spoke through a donkey (Numbers 22:21–39). Peter, on the day of Pentecost, was filled with the Spirit and spoke what God led him to. Even Jesus only spoke what the Father told Him (John 12:49).

Not only does God speak through us, but He also directs our plans. In 1 Samuel 29–30, David is living with the Philistines. Saul is king and wants David dead. The Philistines are going to battle against Israel. But the leaders of the Philistine army do not want David to fight with them as he is an Israelite. They worry he will turn against them. So David goes home. But while he and his men were gone, the Amalekites attacked their city, Ziklag. They burned it and took all the women and children. Therefore, David and his men went to rescue their families from the Amalekites. They fought against them and had victory. Meanwhile, in the other battle, Saul and his sons, including Jonathan, were killed.

Imagine what it would have been like if David had stayed and fought with the Philistines against Israel. First, he would have never known about the attack against Ziklag. He and his men would not have been able to rescue their families. In addition, he would have been on the enemy side of the battle that killed Saul and Jonathan. For years, David had chosen not to put a hand on Saul even when he had the opportunity to kill him. By the rejection of the Philistines, God spared David from the guilt and reputation of having been a part of Saul's and Jonathan's death. *Teach your kids: God is sovereign.*

The Lord weighs the motives (16:2). God will punish even the sins of the heart—arrogance (16:5). God sees the reasons for our actions. He can judge perfectly because He knows our hearts. Sin starts in the heart. Sometimes, Tim and I confess things to each other that we are struggling with. It usually goes something like this: "I am going to tell you this because God already knows what I am thinking." We can take comfort that God knows already, and so it is okay to confess.

We are not surprising Him. We can have comfort that when we are wronged, God will take care of the punishment.

Teach your kids: God is omniscient—all-knowing. God is just.

Commit your works to the Lord and your plans will be established (16:3). When Joshua was entering the promised land, each time he faced a decision concerning who to go up against, he consulted God. The one time he did not was when the Gibeonites tricked them (Joshua 9). Joshua is an example of committing our works to the Lord. In everything you do, consult Him and commit your work unto Him.

Teach your kids: God is faithful.

The Lord has made everything for its own purpose (answer), even the wicked for the day of evil (16:4). The word for the purpose here is the same one used in Proverbs 16:1 for the word answer: *The answer of the tongue is from the LORD.* It is also the same word for the answer in Proverbs 15:1: *A gentle answer turns away wrath.* The idea is to answer or respond. It could be said like this: "God has made everything for its own answer or response. The answer for the wicked is punishment." Everything has its place and order with God. There is no surprise or inconsistency with Him. When you commit wickedness, the answer is judgment. You cannot get away with evil where God is concerned. He is just.

Teach your kids: God is immutable—unchanging and just.

The fear of the Lord will keep you away from evil (16:6). When you put God in the right place, you receive benefits. When you fear God, you will want to avoid evil and its consequences. You will stay away from people who will lead you astray. You will not want to cheat justice. You will work hard. You will use your tongue to build others up. A lifestyle of fearing God will keep you away from the consequences of sin, which leads to extra pain and hurt.

Teach your kids: God is good.

God will even make your enemies to be at peace with you when your ways are pleasing to Him (16:7). Two of my boys were fighting one day. I had to separate them and talk to them individually because things were getting so heated up. As I spoke to one of them, he remarked, "I have to make my brother understand me." Unfortunately, this is not something we can do. God alone has the power to change people. The principle here is that when we obey Him, He can use that to create change in others.

Teach your kids: God changes hearts.

We may have plans, but the Lord directs our steps (16:9). Have you ever had something work out that you never thought would? Or can you think of a situation where everything fell into step? We make plans and try our hardest to accomplish things. We tried for years to get pregnant and to adopt. We tried fertility treatments, injections, and hormones, and nothing happened. We tried adoption. We were picked by three different moms, and each time, the moms changed their minds. Then after four years, I started feeling different. I was pregnant! God will open the door, or the windows, in His time. Consult God in your plans.

Teach your kids: God is sovereign. He is infinite.

God blesses those who trust in Him (16:20). Regardless of the situation or people we face, we can trust in God. He blesses those who trust Him. Sometimes, the blessing is the confidence of being in Him. The blessing can be a peace that passes understanding. Putting our ways, thoughts, and circumstances in His hands will bring us blessings.

Teach your kids: God is merciful.

The lot is cast into the lap, but its every decision is from the Lord (16:33). The lot was one way people made decisions in ancient times. They would use something like rocks or sticks and mark one of them differently. They would then pull one out to make a decision. Here again, Solomon is appealing to his son to realize that God is sovereign. We may think that something is up to chance, but God works things out the way He wants.

Teach your kids: God is omnipotent—all-powerful.

If we look at the attributes that Solomon brings out about God, we can see that some are attributes that separate God from us. Only God is sovereign. Only God can weigh the hearts of men and change them. Only God can control the decision of the lot. He alone is all-powerful and all-knowing. Why does Solomon stop and go over all these attributes of God? I think in the midst of showing his son which way to go and which way is best in life, he wants to remind him of the reasons. We don't do the right thing to look better. We don't do it to get rewards. We don't do it to feel superior to others. We do the right thing because it is what God wants. It is valuable that we stop in the midst of these conversations with our kids and speak to them about the motivation. The ultimate motivation for doing these things is God.

The day may come when our kids will not care about spankings, time-outs, grounding, or lost privileges. They may come to a point where they will take the punishment and not want to do what you ask and submit to you. That is why we must appeal to God as the authority to obey. He is the motivation for right thinking, feeling, and behaving.

What do we learn about God?	What does that mean for us?
He is sovereign.	Everything depends on Him.
He is just.	We should rely on Him.
He rewards and blesses.	There is comfort when we see injustice.
He has a plan.	We should act within the
He sees all.	scope where He blesses.
He is purposeful.	We should align our plans with His.
	We have accountability.
	There is a reason for everything.

Concluding prayer

> Dear Lord,
>
> You are so great and good! You are in control. You give us life and breath. You are the rewarder and giver of blessings. Help me to trust in You, to be led by You, and to honor You in all I do. Help me to see that You are the motivator and reason I should do the right thing. Help me to teach my children that You are sovereign and that Your ways are best. In Jesus's name, amen.

Verse to pray: Ecclesiastes 12:13–14

Practical Proverbs for the family

Use the list of God's attributes for the exercises:

- Immutable—unchanging
- Omnipotent—all-powerful
- Omnipresent—all-present
- Omniscient—all-knowing
- Holy
- Just
- Loving
- Gracious
- Merciful
- Good
- Infinite
- Self-sufficient
- Wise
- Faithful
- Glorious

The naive
- Read Bible Stories that clearly show God's attributes. Here are some examples:

    o Exodus 5–12: Plagues over Egypt
    o Joshua 5–6: Entering the promised land
    o 1 Samuel 16: God chooses David to be king
    o 2 Samuel 7: David's plan to build the temple; God's plan to make a house for David
    o Book of Esther
    o Daniel 1, 3, 4, 5, 6: God's sovereignty over nations, kings, and punishment

The youth and wise
- Where are you reading in the Bible? As you read, look for attributes of God. What do you learn about Him?

Parent reflection and application

- Bring out the character of God in situations in your life. Share instances where God showed Himself to you in the ways this chapter talks about. Did He work out a plan that was not yours? Did He decide for you by closing/opening doors you couldn't have? Did He work something out in a way that you never would have thought of? Write these down and thank God He is in control.

CHAPTER 12

Anger—
Avoid, Slow, Stop, and Control

> He who is slow to anger is better than the mighty, And
> he who rules his spirit, than he who captures a city.
>
> —Proverbs 16:32

Principle: Anger is to be avoided, slowed down, stopped, and controlled.

I'm sure most moms have yelled at their kids, but I doubt many of you have put a hole in the wall. I wrote this chapter on anger because it is something I am familiar with. I have that one kid with whom I butt heads. He pushes my buttons like no one else does. One day, as we were getting ready to go somewhere, he argued with me about everything. He refused to do anything I asked. I was so overcome with frustration and anger I kicked the wall. And to my surprise and embarrassment, I kicked right through the wall and made a hole. Everyone stopped and looked at me in fear. One of the boys started crying. Then I burst into tears. I grabbed the phone and called Tim. "You wouldn't believe what I just did! I was so mad I kicked the wall and put a hole in it." That moment taught me how much of a problem anger was for me. No matter what my kids do, I shouldn't resort to destroying our home.

According to Noah Webster's 1828 Dictionary, anger is a violent passion of the mind excited by a real or supposed injury. Anger is an emotion, a trigger, that there is a perceived injury or wrong. This doesn't mean it is automatically sinful. You can see an injustice and be angry without sinning, but many times, anger comes when we do not get what we want. We perceive our unmet selfish desires as an injury toward us. Anger is dependent on our definition of right and wrong. Our understanding of God's standard of right versus wrong is key to dealing with anger correctly.

From my study, I've concluded that anger is the emotion shown physically as denoted by the Hebrew words "nose" or "face." Its action comes when we burn with the emotion and are provoked to do something about how we feel. The cause of anger can be righteous or unrighteous. In the righteous instance, it is anger directed toward a wrong defined by God. Righteous anger is toward sin, and it is offensive to God and His holy standard of right and wrong, as when Jesus was angry toward the wrong use of His father's house (see John 2). Unrighteous anger is the feeling toward a wrong defined incorrectly apart from God's holy standard of right and wrong, as when Cain was angry because God did not accept his sacrifice (see Genesis 4). God desired a sacrifice of the firstfruits or the best. Yet Abel had given of his firstfruits, but Cain had not. Cain burned with anger because he did not agree with God's right standard of sacrifice. When it wasn't accepted, he became angry and sinned.

Proverbs teaches us four things to do with anger: recognize it, avoid it, be slow to express it, and control it.

Avoiding anger

Keeping away from strife is an honor for a man, but any fool will quarrel (Proverbs 20:3).

Anger usually goes along with strife. Repeatedly, God says that you do not want to live with someone who is controlled by anger or constantly in strife. Proverbs 21:9 and 19 says, "It is better to live in a corner of a roof or in a desert land than with a contentious woman." You can avoid anger by staying away from trouble, such as gossip, problems you are not part of, and contentious people. When you see anger coming, end the conversation and walk away. Avoid people who start fights. Turn from it as if it were a plague.

Be slow to anger

He who is slow to anger has great understanding, but he who is quick-tempered exalts folly (Proverbs 14:29).

According to these verses, to be slow to anger, you need to have understanding. Proverbs 19:11 says you also need discretion, and Proverbs 16:32 mentions self-control ("rules his spirit"). We learned that understanding comes in the second step of our growth into God's way. First comes knowledge—the facts. Understanding is when we get the meaning. Most people know that anger and its reactions are not good (blowing up, yelling, violence, etc.). We have the facts. We have understanding when our being is sold on the fact and can act on it.

We use two phrases in our home when anger starts to rise up. In John 2:13–17, Jesus was angry and drove the merchants out of the temple. Read the passage and note what Jesus did. He saw the people in the temple selling and using His father's house for something it was not intended for. We have this picture of Jesus running through and overthrowing tables and yelling at everyone. But if we look closely, the Bible says He sat down and made a whip. He stopped and braided a whip. He took time before He reacted to the wrong He saw. The whip was likely to drive out the animals. From this story, we use the phrase, "Braid your whip." When angry, we ask each other to just stop.

Discretion makes us slow to anger. Discretion is to have insight, to ponder or consider. Being "slow to anger" stops the reaction, so we can take a few moments to use discretion and reasoning. The other phrase or picture we use is "Let it get from the back to the front" (credit for this is from *Relational Wisdom* and Ken Sande).[1] We point

---

[1] Ken Sande, "Relational Wisdom 360—Going Beyond Emotional Intelligence Online Training Study Guide," rw360.org (2018), 9, https://rw360.org/wp-content/uploads/2020/10/DRW-2.0-Study-Guide-Partial.pdf.

to the back of our heads and then to the front. The hypothalamus is in the back of your brain. It is where you perceive feelings and receive sensory input. This is where you see a wrong done or recognize that you are not getting your way, and the experience is processed into your brain. The frontal lobe of your brain, in your forehead, is where decision-making is done. Here is where you weigh the sensory input and formulate a plan on what to do with it. Many times, if we wait and let it get from the back (the hypothalamus) to the frontal lobe, we can reason and ponder if the reaction is worth the consequence. This only takes a few seconds.

Being slow to anger is a form of self-control. Proverbs speaks about it as a man who rules his spirit. To rule your spirit, you must know it. You must know yourself, your weaknesses, and your triggers to anger. What sets you off? What bothers you? What do you desire that, when you don't get it, you become angry? Self-control starts with self-awareness.

Dealing with current anger

Proverb's prescription:
As I struggled with anger, the Lord convicted me of this verse in James 1:20: "The anger of man does not achieve the righteousness of God." I will not lead my son closer to God by using anger. To accomplish righteousness and lead him closer to God, I need God's ways of dealing with anger. God showed me a battle plan to deal with it: self-control, gentle words, and a gift.

A gentle word turns away wrath, but a harsh word stirs up anger (Proverbs 15:1).

A gift in secret subdues anger, and a bribe in the bosom, strong wrath (Proverbs 21:14).

I wasn't sure what this second verse meant, and for a while, I ignored it. I just won't use that or talk about it, I thought. But eventually, in studying every reference to anger, I had to deal with it. The idea is to give a gift to the angry person. Remember, anger is passion in the mind when someone has felt injustice. To quench anger, we can repair the injury felt by giving the perpetrator a gift. They feel like they have lost something, so replace what they feel they've lost.

We are not giving a physical gift but a gift of a calm spirit, mercy, understanding, or a listening ear. Have you ever been with a person who is angry and after they have exploded, they calmed down and became a different person? My son, who deals with anger, is the sweetest, most thoughtful person. But when he is angry, he slams doors, kicks anything in his way, pushes, and even gets physical with people. He has even said, "I only say those things when I am angry, Mom. I don't mean them." I know when I am angry, I have said things I do not mean and done things I did not want to do (like kicking a hole in the wall).

This verse that I avoided for so long was what God used to help deal with my anger. Once when my son was angry, God got a hold of my heart. He told me to go up and hold him. I wiped his tears, embraced him, and told him how much I loved him and that I wanted to help him deal with this anger. He almost immediately calmed down. It was a gift of peace to him. He still had to deal with the consequences of how he had treated his brother and me. He had to reconcile the relationships and ask for forgiveness. But the anger subsided with the gift.

The next phrase in the verse gives an even better picture: *"A bribe in the bosom subdues wrath."* I love it! The idea of a bribe is that it usually is used to pervert justice. Someone gives a bribe to get their verdict. The bribe changes the outcome. Here, the bribe is used to prevent anger. It changes the goal of anger to get a peaceful verdict. Instead of going to the judge to give him a bribe to turn justice the wrong way, you go to the angry person to give him a gift to turn their anger in a peaceful way. I love doing this! I have dealt with people who are angry and given them the gift of a listening ear. I once bought a material gift for a person who was angry. I knew she felt wronged. I love seeing the countenance of an angry person change. With man's ways, when someone is angry, we usually give back anger, and a fight ensues. Or we try to convince them that their anger is not valid. When we do this, we are saying that their perceived hurt is wrong. God can deal with the hurt, and He can convict if the wrong is perceived or selfish. With God's ways, anger is turned away with gentle words and gifts.

Anger is inevitable. Here is a strategy based on God's way that will help keep relationships intact, be a witness to those around you, and ultimately honor the Lord. We need to be prepared for conflict and strife so we can do as Ephesians 4:26–27 says, "Be angry, and yet do not sin; do not let the sun go down on your anger, and do not give the devil an opportunity." Be battle-ready, and do not give the devil a place in your territory with anger. If you do not have a strategy, anger will come in, and the devil will get into the hole in your weak wall.

Practical Proverbs anger battle plan

1. Avoid it. Avoid the person who makes trouble and the fight you see brewing.
2. Be slow to it. Braid your whip.
3. Have discretion. Take a few seconds to consider "Let it get from the back to the front."
4. Rule your spirit/have self-control.
5. Use gentle words and gifts to bribe anger away and stop the stirring.

Concluding prayer

> Dear Lord,
>
> Please help me to be slow to anger and to avoid it. Help me to be aware and recognize and see the hurts that so often cause anger. Help me to guide my children in these concepts. Help us not to be angry with each other and, when we are, to restore our relationships. Please help us to be ruled by the fruit of self-control that only You can give through Your Spirit. In Jesus's name, amen.
>
> Verse to pray: Ephesians 4:26

Practical Proverbs for the family

The naive
- *Recognize anger.* What does it look like when someone is angry? Act out someone who is angry (stomping feet, yelling, grunting, etc.). What does it look like when someone is at peace?
- *Face game.* Have the child guess if you are angry, sad, happy, surprised, etc. This helps them to recognize nonverbal communication in people. Let them do it, and you guess.

The youth
- Talk about anger.
- What is it?
- What makes you angry?
- What do you do when you are angry?
- Read the story of David, Abigail, and Nabal in 1 Samuel 25. Who was angry? At what were they angry? How was anger turned away? How was sin avoided?

The wise
- Read James 1:19–20 and James 4:1–3. What causes dissension and fights? What is the root?
- How do we know when anger is sinful or righteous? Read John 2 and Isaiah 53. Can you identify what the anger was directed at in these passages? What does it tell you about righteous anger?

Parent reflection and application

- List each person in your family. Observe when they get angry. Learn what is the hurt that causes the anger and what is it that person values that, when lost, causes them to be angry. How can you help them identify it and stop it before it happens? How can you turn away the anger?

CHAPTER 13

Words and the Tongue

> Death and life are in the power of the tongue,
> and those who love it will eat its fruit.
>
> —Proverbs 18:21

Principle: The tongue either builds or tears down, either produces life or destroys it.

I wasn't sure about including this chapter. This is actually the last chapter I added to the book, but when I looked at the study I had done and counted all the instances of the words tongue, words, mouth, and lips, I saw that it is mentioned eighty times in Proverbs. This section, chapters 10–24, has over 70 percent of the instances of the tongue, so this should probably be included. Proverbs 18:21 says, "Death and life are in the power of the tongue, and those who love it will eat its fruit."

We live a block from the river. When we moved to our home, I knew things grew better because the river was near. The grass is greener. There are more trees. Many people have gardens, but I was surprised by how much animal life there was down in the Albuquerque valley. Within the first summer there, we encountered toads, snakes, bats, coyotes, mice, raccoons, owls, skunks, geese, ducks, and even a river otter. This is besides the homes with farm animals. That water was near meant there was life.

We don't often think of where our water comes from because of our modern conveniences. This past summer, the pump on our well broke, and it took a few weeks to fix it. It was difficult to go from automatic watering to having to hand water everything on our property. Imagine living life when you had to walk down with a jar to get your water from the well every day. Proverbs says that our words are a fountain of life. They are like springs that provide water for the basic needs of life.

Life produces. Death stops things. Our words should produce life by feeding, delivering, healing, and making the heart glad. The right words can heal a broken heart. A gentle word can turn away anger. Good news can put fat on the bones. The right words can spring life into another and lift their soul. Our words can have a literal physical effect on another person. I like to think of it like this: my words should produce something in others. They should produce growth in relationships, courage in others, and praise for God.

The night I graduated from high school, I went with a few friends for ice cream and then went home. I did not go to any of the parties afterward because the next morning, I was getting up early to go on a mission trip. That night, one of my teachers approached me. He handed me a $100 bill to put toward my trip. He told me I had a special opportunity and gift to serve others cross-culturally because I spoke Spanish. He said that I could connect with people in a deeper way than someone like him could because of this and that I should use that ability for God. Those words stuck with me. They gave me a drive and a challenge to take seriously what I was doing. His words lifted me up and gave me the courage to go speak to people I did not know about the gospel. They were life-giving words.

Conversely, that same summer, I worked for a woman who ran her own business. She made soaps, lotions, and candles in her home. She hired me to do some of the detailed work of putting soaps in little cloth bags, tying bows, wrapping, and packaging the products. I ended up not being very good at it. My bows were different sizes. I was too slow for her production, so she fired me. But in the process of firing me, she asked me what I wanted to do with my life. I responded that I wanted to go into the music business. Well, she told me that I should probably find something else to do because I was not cut out for business. Those words stuck with me: "You should find something else to do. You are not good at business." Not being good at tying small bows or packing things does not mean you are bad at business. She could have encouraged me to find a different type of work. Her words were not life-giving.

Safe and enjoyable talk

Proverbs describes life-giving words as *gentle, sweet, soothing*, and *pleasant*. When I teach my kids about the word gentle, I demonstrate how we touch a baby's face. We gently stroke their cheek. We have the power to slap a baby, but we would never do that! We restrain that power and use gentle strokes to touch the baby. Now we apply that to words. Do we want to slap others with our words or gently stroke them?

To teach the word "sweet," I get out any candy or treat. These are things we like. Sweetness appeals to us, and so should sweet words. Someone is more likely to listen to sweet words than harsh words. Our words should be like a sweet treat or candy in the ears of others.

We love camping. And one of our favorite things to do is hang a hammock up between two trees in the forest and just rest. Lying in a hammock is soothing. It gently moves and makes you feel relaxed. Your eyes blink or stare off into space. The rhythm makes your head droop down. It is the complete opposite of a roller coaster. Soothing words should relax someone, making them feel at ease and safe. Do people feel safe with your talk? I know someone I don't like to be around because they always criticize and complain. I sometimes tense up when I know I will have to go talk to them. We do not want people to feel that way about us.

Pleasantness is something we enjoy. A pleasant sound is a concert we enjoy, something we want to hear. An unpleasant sound is the high-pitched smoke alarm that goes off when we make bacon and burn the grease. You would not want to listen to that for an hour, but you would listen to a concert of your favorite music for an hour. Pleasant words are words that others enjoy. They are glad to hear your words.

Others-focused talk

One thing I notice about people is what they talk about. I notice how many times people will talk about themselves versus asking questions to learn about another person. I think about someone I interacted with for five years. I kept track, and not once did they ever ask me a question in conversation, not even "How are you?" They always talked about themselves. The next step in life-giving words is to have conversations that are not self-centered.

What we talk about shows who and what we care about. It reveals our priorities. Do we always want to tell our side of the story? Or vent about something? Do we demonstrate interest in others by asking questions about them? Do we want to hear about their day?

Just as right and timely words can heal and bring life, wrong words can bring ruin and destroy. Proverbs list flatterers, slanderers, liars, whisperers, and the perverse among the category of people that destroy with their words: There is one who speaks rashly like the thrust of a sword (Proverbs 12:18). These are some of the types of speech that tear down and cause trouble according to Proverbs: gossip, miscommunication, communicating information without having all the facts, slander, hate speech, joking, judging, and lying.

"By the blessing of the upright a city is exalted, but by the mouth of the wicked it is torn down" (Proverbs 11:11).

"A gentle answer turns away wrath" (Proverbs 15:1).

"Sweetness of speech increases persuasiveness" (Proverbs 16:21).

"Like apples of gold in settings of silver is a word spoken in right circumstances" (Proverbs 25:11).

Commands regarding the tongue and words

We are to *guard* our tongue. Guard it as if it were a prisoner trying to escape. We are to restrain our tongue and know when to keep silent. My husband has a saying, "Just because it is true does not mean it should be said." We are to *give words of life* to others. Finally, we are to *produce* life with our words.

Concluding prayer

> Dear Lord,
>
> Please help me to control my tongue. May my words be life-giving and build others up. May my words produce something in others. Help me with communication that is clear in words, tone, and body language. Help me to teach my children these things. May our home be one where our tongue is pleasing to You. And when not, convict us of our sins and help restore our relationships to each other. In Jesus's name, amen.
>
> Verse to pray: James 1:26

Practical Proverbs for the family

The naive
- Talk about when words hurt you or lifted you up.
- Practice saying encouraging words to others.
- Find ways to restate these phrases. Try using gentleness, sweetness, pleasantness, or soothing speech:
    "Stop it! You are bothering me!"
    "Shut up! I don't want to listen to you."
    "You make me so angry."
    "You always _____."
    "You never _____."

The youth
- Look at the verses about the tongue. What is the power our words/tongue has?

    o   Proverbs 15:1
    o   Proverbs 15:23
    o   Proverbs 15:30

- Proverbs 16:24
- Proverbs 16:28
- Proverbs 17:27
- Proverbs 17:28
- Proverbs 18:13
- Proverbs 21:23

The wise
- Look at the verses about the tongue. Give a real-life example for each.

Parent reflection and application

- Give true, specific words of affirmation to your children regularly. Tell them what they are good at, why you like them, and that you are glad they are yours.
- Encourage gratitude. Talk about things you are thankful for.

SECTION 3: COMPLETE INDEPENDENCE

Skill with Responsibilities— The Adviser Stage

> By wisdom a house is built, and by understanding
> it is established; and by knowledge the rooms are
> filled with all precious and pleasant riches.
>
> —Proverbs 24:3–4

The final stage of childhood is the teen years. Knowledge makes life pretty, the furnishings that will fill and decorate a life. Understanding makes life steady and strong. But ultimately, wisdom is what will build a skillful life.

As I wrote this, part of my time was taken up talking to someone who was struggling with relationships. Why can't people honor their commitments? Why can't they recognize truth and love? It was one of those moments where you know the person isn't really asking for answers. They just want someone to listen. Why do people have such a problem with relationships? Why do we have trouble being disciplined in carrying through on our commitments? The answer is simple. We don't do it God's way.

Relationships, commitments, and work ethic—all require wisdom. A teenager who lacks perspective needs wisdom. A child who throws a fit because they don't want to eat vegetables needs wisdom. A man who keeps attaching himself to the wrong woman needs wisdom. The person addicted to substances and the employee who lacks self-management skills need wisdom. It all comes down to God's ways. His ways are best and bring blessings. His ways help men and women carry through with commitments and ask forgiveness when they have broken them. God's wisdom gives us the ability to relate to others, to communicate, to be merciful, to hold our tongues when needed, to use a gentle answer to turn away wrath, to work hard and enjoy the fruits of our labor, to receive instruction and grow, to have integrity and honesty, to not be overcome with substances, to manage business, to shepherd churches, to run governments with justice, to build our homes and not tear them down.

This section is the shortest. If we have read, understood, and practiced the first two sections of Proverbs, this part will just add to what we have already done. This is the last tier of the foundation we lay. Let's review. In chapters 1–9, we laid the foundation for authority and obedience through the fear of the Lord, the basic relational skill of listening, the ability to recognize and gain wisdom, and the capability of discerning to beware of bad company. We are repeating and instructing all the time.

During the second stage, we converse about the two ways of life by comparing God's way, or the wise way, with man's way, the foolish way. We are bringing out what the character of each looks like. We are inspired or motivated by God's lasting rewards and authority.

In this final stage, we are advising and adding to all that has been instructed on and talked about. Solomon's son will have a position of authority. He will be king. Kindness, integrity, and compassion are lived out through the management of people. Lying lips, honesty, and justice are discussed in the realm of judging and ruling. Working hard and attaining wealth is looked at from a more lasting perspective of leaving an inheritance for those after you. What is discussed grows to how it affects others and how it should be used by one in a position of authority.

Look back at the goals in Proverbs 1:5–6. The goal for this stage is that the wise increase in learning, the man of understanding acquires wise counsel, that he understands a proverb, a figure, the words of the wise, and a riddle. The focus of this stage is threefold. First, to build upon what has been taught. Second, to help our children not only recognize wisdom but to seek wisdom and wise people. Finally, their skill in discernment should be honed to be quicker and more accurate.

The cultural element is significant to note here. This section of Proverbs (chapters 25–31) was intended for older children entering adulthood. In the Hebrew culture, a boy became a man at twelve years of age. They prepared for the adulthood stage of vocation, marriage, family, and responsibility. Our society delays adulthood and has created a stage between childhood and adulthood, but this did not exist in the Hebrew culture.

One thing we have missed in our culture, especially in the last few generations, is the preparation for adulthood. Society has decided that we should be proud of ourselves for "adulting." As a child's job is to obey, listen, and learn, an adult's job is to hold responsibility and manage it. We have not been preparing our children for this, and we must. Discussing and preparing our children for the responsibilities of adulthood is an important stage of raising them. Let's look at the content of what we advise and how.

The four Ws of a man's adulthood

In this last section, Solomon tells his son how to become a leader who manages his wine, his workers, his wealth, and his woman. In this stage, we are preparing to let go of our children, that they be the managers of their own lives, homes, relationships, and responsibilities. Parents are to be advisers in this stage of life. In this section, the receiver of the information is not "my son" or "a man" but "the king." The phrase "the king" or "ruler" is mentioned seventeen times in these last chapters. Solomon is preparing his son to be a ruler or manager of people. Proverbs 31 mentions that a woman looks well to the ways of her house. She is a manager. In this section, we hear from other men besides Solomon. Note that chapter 25 contains the Proverbs of Hezekiah, which his men transcribed. Also, chapter 30 notes the words of Agur: an oracle or burden. Chapter 31 is written by King Lemuel from the words his mother taught him.

CHAPTER 14

Wine and Drunkenness

> Your eyes will see strange things and your
> mind will utter perverse things.
>
> —Proverbs 23:33

Principle: Overconsumption of wine affects us physically and mentally, thereby affecting our relationships, responsibilities, and ability to manage well.

I grew up in a small town in Spain where wine was a source of income for people. When I was little, my best friend and I were playing at the house of someone with a vineyard. Our parents were talking, and we went to explore and found the wine cellar. A little while later, our parents found us soaked in wine, our clothes stained red. Alcohol is part of life for many people. In Scripture, wine was used for a lot of things. It was part of the sacrifices and celebrations. It was part of their diet, as often throughout history, wine was more accessible and healthier than water. But it was also a problem for those who let themselves be controlled by it.

Chapters 23 and 31 cover wine and drunkenness. Proverbs 23:29 starts with several questions: "Who has woes, sorrows, contentions, complaining, wounds without cause and redness of eyes?" The answer: "Those who linger long over wine." The one who lingers is not anyone who drinks some wine. If you have a glass of wine, you will not have sorrows and woes. Lingering is procrastinating, taking longer than needed, delaying, and hindering by delaying. This person is staying with wine as a companion, and it is affecting them mentally and physically. Solomon uses a different kind of approach here by giving the consequences first in the form of a question. He is asking his son, "Do you want all these bad consequences?" Then he tells them what the consequences consist of.

He starts with the question and answers right off. Why would you want to drink wine? Obviously, people do, so he then explains why. The answer is that it is tempting and physically appealing. The wine looks good, it tastes good, it feels good. "Do not look on the wine when it is red, when it sparkles in the cup, when it goes down smoothly" (Proverbs 23:31). The sparkly wine he speaks of is wine that has been fermented twice. It has more sugar in it. Therefore, it tastes good. Remember, these people did not have candy bars and brownies. The wine appeals to their sweet tooth. It is pleasurable. The color of the wine even looks good. And when you drink it, it goes down smoothly. Again, remember there were no Starbucks frappuccinos, no Keva Juice smoothies, and no Sonic Icees. Wine was refreshing.

But the pleasure is temporary. "At the last it bites like a serpent and stings like a viper" (Proverbs 23:32). Listen to the symptoms of a common snake bite. There is swelling around the bite, fever, headache, convulsions, and numbness. A venomous snake bite can cause dizziness, weakness, headache, blurred vision, excessive sweating, fever, thirst, nausea, vomiting, fainting, and convulsions. Solomon must have seen some snake bites in his life!

The symptoms are similar to a person who is intoxicated. They have headaches, blackouts, dehydration, flushing, nausea, vomiting, rapid involuntary eye movement, blurred vision, problems with coordination, drowsiness, and seizures. Proverbs 23:33–35: "Your eyes will see strange things and your mind will utter perverse things. And you will be like one who lies down in the middle of the sea, or like one who lies down on the top of a mast. They struck me, but I did not become ill; they beat me, but I did not know it. When shall I awake? I will seek another drink." The symptoms of intoxication or lingering long over wine are similar to those of a snake bite. In a way,

Solomon is asking, "Would you ever, purposefully, let a snake bite you? Then why would you get drunk?"

He goes on to tell his son that his senses will not perceive correctly. He is likely to make bad decisions from bad sensory input. Then he describes these bad decisions: "You will lie down on a mast or the middle of the sea." Think of all the areas of life: relationships, finances, education, vocation, spiritual, physical, recreational, and personal. If you cannot decide where to properly lie down, how will you make decisions in these areas?

When lingering long over wine, there is physical sickness, then mental instability. Finally, complete numbness and emotional breakdown appear. Solomon describes it: "They struck me, but I did not become ill; they beat me, but I did not know it. When shall I awake? I will seek another drink" (Proverbs 23:35). He is mistreated and abused without having the basic sense of preservation and self-defense. He has become numb to the world around him. Numbness is the ultimate low point in someone's life. It is the point of despair, not caring, not feeling anymore. Life becomes nothing more than seeking another drink. There is addiction and complete dependency. Why would one ever want to live like this? God is warning us of the way of the fool that leads to physical ailments, mental blurriness, emotional breakdown, and complete despair through addiction. God does not desire this for us, and we should not desire it for our children. We must warn them! We must have this conversation!

Proverbs 31:4–7 is the other main passage, and they are the words of a mama to her son, the king. She tells him it is not appropriate for kings to drink or desire strong drinks. And again, she explains why. We cannot just give commands to our grown children. They must understand in order to be able to use the knowledge on their own. So she tells him that the reason is that he might forget what is decreed and pervert the rights of the people. Drunkenness affects judgment, decision-making, and discernment.

Do you know the story of Esther? Remember when Queen Vashti is asked to come to the party of the king? King Ahasuerus had conquered Greece and wanted to celebrate. He had been celebrating for several months. The king and his friends would get drunk during these celebrations, and they would discuss laws, policies, and ideas. Many times, they made decisions while intoxicated. I believe that is what happened with Vashti. The king and his advisers were sitting around drunk at this party, and they wanted some extra entertainment, so they asked Vashti to come. When Vashti refused, the king and his advisers discussed this affront and made a new law (Esther 1).

King Lemuel's mother is warning him about this because he has a responsibility to the people under him to keep his judgment and his discernment pure. Look at what she says in verses 8–9, "Open your mouth for the mute, for the rights of all the unfortunate. Open your mouth, judge righteously, and defend the rights of the afflicted and needy." It is as if she is literally saying, "Open your mouth to produce something good, not consume something bad." Are you in a position that affects others and their wellbeing? Are you in a position of responsibility? The substances you put in your body should not affect your ability to judge and make decisions for those for whom you are responsible.

We must look at verses 6–7 to make sure they are not misunderstood: "Give strong drink to him who is perishing, And wine to him whose life is bitter. Let him drink and forget his poverty and remember his trouble no more." Is King Lemuel's mom permitting drunkenness if we are poor or want to forget life? I believe the point being made is that King Lemuel, one in authority, should not at all use wine to the point of drunkenness. He is the complete opposite of one who is perishing, bitter, and poor. Remember that Proverbs is Hebrew poetry and uses parallelism, comparison, and contrast to make a point. King Lemuel's mom is making a hyperbolic comparison here.

Since addiction leads to numbness and despair, it will only add to that condition. I believe she is trying to make a point of last resort: if anyone would get drunk, let him be this guy! She is not saying this guy should. She is making a point that the king has so much responsibility, so much going for him, that he cannot afford to do this.

On the other hand, this allowance was included in Scripture. What is the point of letting this person drink? To let him forget and remember no more. When things get bad enough, are we given permission to numb the pain or to forget with a substance? Look at what situations King Lemuel's mom mentions: one who is perishing, one whose life is bitter, and one who is in poverty. Let's look at those three situations.

The word for perishing is one who is destroyed or dying. Remember, there were no anesthetics back then. Alcohol was used as a painkiller throughout history before the invention of modern drugs. The word for "bitter" is the same word Ruth's mother-in-law, Naomi, used. She had lost her husband and two sons. Back then, a woman was valued for the children she produced. Without a man in her life, she had no means of sustaining herself financially. Naomi is an example of a bitter life.

The last, one who is in poverty, may not be as bad as the first two, but think of biblical examples of poor people. Think of Job, who lost everything and sat at the gates in rags. The poor were at the mercy of their neighbors and those around them. There were no soup kitchens, government assistance programs, or food pantries in those days. But even if one is in a situation like this and drinks excessively to where it will help him forget his troubles, it is still only a temporary solution. Proverbs 23:35 ends with "When shall I awake? I will seek another drink." It doesn't solve the problem of death, despair, bitterness, or poverty. It never satisfies.

On the contrary, if we are in Christ, He calls us victorious. He says we have abundant life. We abide in Him, the maker of the universe and our bodies. We are conquerors, overcomers, and free. No matter what terrible situations we have faced, Christ says that He gives us His Spirit, which raised Jesus from the dead. God says He will never leave us nor forsake us. He will pull us out of the pit. He will walk with us through the valley of the shadow of death. He holds our tears in a bottle. He takes account of our wanderings. If you feel you are in the deepest part of life, know that Jesus is there. God cares for you. There are so many things He has provided to help us through dark times.

Here is a list of the exact prohibitions:

- Don't be with heavy drinkers of wine (Proverbs 23:20, the influence of others).

- Do not look on the wine (Proverbs 23:31, the temptation of pleasure).
- Do not give your ways to that which destroys kings (Proverbs 31:3, the effect on responsibility).

Concluding prayer

Dear Lord,

Please help me to not be controlled by drunkenness. Help me to avoid situations of temptation. Help me not to give my strength away to being drunk as it will control my life. Help me to communicate these truths to my children. In Jesus's name, amen.

Verse to pray: Ephesians 5:18

Practical Proverbs for the family

Because this section is for the wise, older kids, I have not included practical things for younger children. The focus for them is the earlier part in Proverbs. But this does not mean you cannot read it to them or find a verse you can use.

The wise
- Look up the symptoms of intoxication and compare them to the picture Solomon gives in Proverbs 23:29–35.
- Go through each area of life. How would being intoxicated affect your decisions? What would drunkenness look like if put before…
    - personal—your own discipline and habits
    - relational—friends, spouse, children
    - recreational—enjoyment of other activities such as sports or art

- vocational—responsibilities at work
- educational—growth and learning
- physical—exercise and health
- spiritual—relationship with God

• Look up the following verses about who we are in Christ and what He does for us in the midst of difficulties.

- Psalm 23
- Psalm 56
- John 10:10
- John 15
- 1 John 5:5
- Romans 8:11
- Romans 8:31–39
- Ephesians 3:20

Parents

• Discuss substance abuse with your kids.
• Read through the passages and answer the following questions. Write them down. Writing helps you organize your thoughts and ideas so you can more clearly communicate them to others.

What does Proverbs say about the effect of alcohol?
What does it say about the temptation of alcohol?
What does it say about the instances where you can drink alcohol?
What are the exact prohibitions in Proverbs?

CHAPTER 15

Workers—
The Skill of Managing and Leading People

> Those who forsake the law praise the wicked, but
> those who keep the law strive with them.
>
> —Proverbs 28:4

Principle: The wise person will manage and influence others with kindness, truth, and justice.

Proverbs 25–31 are the last chapters of the book. They seem random, but at closer inspection, you can see the person he is speaking about. These chapters include the king, neighbor, enemy, contentious woman, fool, sluggard, poor and rich, friend, flocks, children, and wife. Solomon is clearly talking to someone who is not a child anymore. The recipient has more responsibility. He is talking to someone who is a leader, someone who has neighbors and enemies. The man is looking for a wife. He has children and flocks. He needs to know about being rich and poor. It is clearly someone growing into more responsibility.

Leadership

First Kings 10 tells the account of the Queen of Sheba visiting Solomon. You can read that she observes the wisdom of his court and notices there was wisdom in the seating of his servants, the attendance of his waiters, and his cupbearers. Solomon's wisdom was not just for himself; it extended to the management of his court and the people who worked for him. As one grows in wisdom, that wisdom should extend to the relationships one manages.

One of the best bosses I ever had was my father-in-law. I interned in the youth ministry of the church he pastored. He was a good boss because he knew my strengths and weaknesses. Therefore, he put me in a position where I excelled. In addition, he knew that I was hardworking and independent. He set clear expectations for my job duties and then allowed me to tackle them on my own. My boss did not micromanage me, for he knew that I was self-motivated, so he let me set my own timelines, deadlines, and goals. He knew that if I needed help, I would ask for it. Besides, he trusted my work because he had trained me.

A wise leader will teach, train, and give opportunities for those under him to work and be tested. Jesus did this with His disciples. He chose them and trained them for three years. He taught them and gave them insights and explanations that He did not share with the crowds. The disciples observed Jesus at work, and then He tested them. During those three years, He sent them out twice to minister to the cities of Israel.

A similar sequence should happen with parents and children. Teach them what they need to know. Train them by practicing it often. Then let them try it out. This is the stage the son is at in this last section of Proverbs.

A wise leader has certain characteristics, according to Proverbs. First, he has counselors: "By wise guidance you will wage war, and in abundance of counselors there is victory" (Proverbs 24:6). Leaders should always be growing and learning because they are making decisions for others. They need to have good judgment and know right and wrong. I am the director of a homeschool group. When I have to make big decisions for the group, I always consult two or three mentors and pray.

Additionally, a wise leader listens to his people and is aware of what is going on. He checks in and pays attention. Proverbs 27:23 says, "Know well the condition of your flocks." To "know the condition" is to know their face.

My sons take care of our chickens. I can't tell them all apart, but my sons are good managers of them, for they know the temperaments of each chicken. The boys know which ones are mean, which ones like to escape the coop, and which ones will peck your face!

Moreover, a wise leader uses justice. Proverbs 24:24–25 says, "He who says to the wicked, 'You are righteous,' peoples will curse him, nations will abhor him; but to those who rebuke the wicked will be delight, and a good blessing will come upon them." Solomon asked God for wisdom in leading Israel. He specifically asked that God would help him discern right from wrong so he could judge well. Justice, the knowledge of right and wrong applied to situations with people, is important in leading others.

There is an emphasis in this section on listening to the law or the Torah. The Torah was God's standard of right and wrong. He is not talking about the ceremonial or religious law but the civil law of Israel, the part of the law that concerns man's relationship to each other. God cares a great deal about justice and hates the perversion of it. The Mosaic law was one of the most thorough and fair laws in any ancient culture. God's law had an aspect of restoration that other systems did not have. The Israelites had no prison system. If you wronged someone, you had to make restitution. For example, if you killed your neighbor's ox, you would pay him back with two oxen. The Old Testament law was the first to speak on the different motives and levels of murder—accidental and intentional. There were provisions for men who killed someone accidentally and differing measures of punishment for a motive. God came up with the degrees of murder before man did.

"The exercise of justice is joy for the righteous, But is terror to workers of iniquity" (Proverbs 21:15).

The sad thing is that I don't know if Solomon followed this advice. After he died, Jeroboam and Rehoboam were both pining for the throne. The people asked Rehoboam to be a less harsh king than Solomon was. In 1 Kings 12:4, the people of Israel and Jeroboam petition Rehoboam, "Your father made our yoke hard; now therefore lighten the hard service of your father and his heavy yoke which he put on us, and we will serve you." It sounded like Solomon had not always been just to his people. Even his counselors admit this in verse eight. But just because the writer did not follow this advice does not mean we shouldn't. These are still the words of God.

Social relationships

In chapters 10–15, we looked at the contrast of right and wrong but also the character of the wise and foolish. Now in chapters 25 through 29, these characteristics are mentioned in the context of different social relationships and types of people we will encounter in life. Here is a list:

- Self

    One of the first things it mentions is our own heart problems-pride, boasting, and arrogance. It warns us not to claim honor in front of others or seek our own glory lest we be humbled.

    "Let another praise you, and not your own mouth; a stranger, and not your own lips" (Proverbs 27:2).

- Fool

    There is a repeat of the characteristics of the fool, but this time, it goes into how unreliable the fool is. So not only should we beware of joining or being like the fool, but we should not rely on him. He is not someone you would want to hire in your business. Neither is he someone you should try to teach and instruct. He is not someone you can even converse with. Do not answer the fool.

"He cuts off his own feet and drinks violence who sends a message by the hand of a fool" (Proverbs 26:6).

- Friend

  This section speaks on the characteristics and qualities of a good friend. He will rebuke you and wound you with truth, but he will prove faithful. A friend does not flatter. A friend sharpens you like iron. A good friend cares about you growing in wisdom.

  "Faithful are the wounds of a friend, but deceitful are the kisses of an enemy" (Proverbs 27:6).

- Sluggard

  Like the fool, the sluggard is unreliable. He turns over in his bed. He is too lazy to even feed himself. Do not hire or rely on a lazy person, for they will bring you trouble. Again, this implies that the son is now in a position of ownership or management and is hiring and relying on people.

  "The sluggard buries his hand in the dish; He is weary of bringing it to his mouth again" (Proverbs 26:15).

- The Contentious

  Proverbs 26:17–28 talks about people who are contentious through their words. They whisper, gossip, deceive, joke, flatter, and lie. It also mentions the contentious woman and warns that it is better to live on the corner of the roof than with one like her. Proverbs 26:21 says, "Like charcoal to hot embers and wood to fire, So is a contentious man to kindle strife." Do not build relationships with people who like to fight. You will be miserable. Solomon is not talking about a little squabble. He speaks about repeated habits and a long-term relationship.

  The wise person will manage and influence others with God's relational leadership tools. They will seek counselors. They pay attention to their people. They use their understanding of God's measure of right and wrong to make decisions and judgments. They remember the principle of restoration from God's law. They are wise in choosing the people they build relationships with, whether business, work, or personal.

Concluding prayer

Dear Lord,

Please help me to look at people as You would. Help me to be just and to wisely manage my knowledge of right and wrong. Help me to impress on my children the importance of looking to counselors for wisdom and looking toward others with justice and awareness. Help my children and me to identify the characteristics of wisdom and foolishness in ourselves and others, to be careful to yoke ourselves with the right people. Help us to be humble, knowing we sin and err, and to find forgiveness and healing in You. Help us always to love people as You would. In Jesus's name, amen.

Verse to pray: Proverbs 28:5

Practical Proverbs for the family

Because this section is for the wise, older kids, I have not included practical things for younger children. The focus for them is the earlier part in Proverbs. But this does not mean you cannot read it to them or find a verse you can use.

The wise
- Read through chapters 25–29 and write down what Proverbs says about these categories of people. What are

the qualities and characteristics of each? How should we treat each of them?

- The fool
- The sluggard
- A friend
- A neighbor
- The contentious
- The boastful
- An enemy
- The poor
- The rich
- The law follower

Parent reflection and application

Questions to ask yourself about relationships:

- Does the person seek their own glory?
- Does the person build you up and make you better?
- Does the person allow you to make them better or build up? Or do they always have a response or excuse?
- Do they like to fight or argue? Do they always have to be right or have the last word?
- Have you ever heard the person say they are sorry without conditions or excuses?
- Does the person work hard? Do they complete tasks or assignments they say they will?
- Does the person know what is going on with the area they manage? Are they aware of the needs or feelings of others?
- Do they listen?

CHAPTER 16

Wealth—
The Skill of Managing
Money and Materials

> Give me neither poverty nor riches; feed me with the
> food that is my portion, that I will not be full and deny
> You and say, "Who is the Lord?" Or that I not be in
> want and steal, and profane the name of my God.
>
> —Proverbs 30:8–9

Principle: God is the owner; we are managers. Since it is His, we should acknowledge Him in it and share it with others.

God is the owner; we are managers

A couple of years ago, we purchased a bigger home in the Albuquerque Valley. Tim and I had moved into our previous home before we had any children. We could have stayed there and raised five boys just fine. But as we had our fifth, we started to pray for a home in a more rural area with more outdoor space. We wanted a different lifestyle for our children. Our desire was for time outside in God's creation with space for gardens and animals. We looked at properties and made offers, but none worked out. As we shared that prayer request with others, I was shocked at the Christians who told us to be satisfied with what we had. Their advice was to be content with our current home.

We continued to pray, and I struggled with the question, "Am I content?" So I prayed for contentment. One day, our Realtor sent us a home listing. I didn't like the pictures, and it was over our budget. I didn't want to see it, but he kept insisting. As we drove down the street, I felt like it was the one. We hadn't even gone inside, but the outdoor space was what we had desired and prayed for.

God opened doors so quickly for us. We found a renter for our current home within days. We moved out in less than a month. It is like all those prayers finally got through the enemy's attacks. When I cross the living room from my bedroom to the kitchen, I look out at the yard and thank God for what He gave us. What I have is God's, not mine.

Having enough wealth is subjective. What one person thinks is enough is not enough for someone else. I have found that our ideas of money are ingrained in how we grew up and in the culture around us instead of what the Bible teaches. Proverbs 30:8–9 says, "Give me neither poverty nor riches; Feed me with the food that is my portion, That I will not be full and deny You and say, 'Who is the Lord?' Or that I not be in want and steal, And profane the name of my God." The writer wants just enough, but why? He wants neither extreme riches nor poverty. He wants to acknowledge God in his need but not fall into sin in his want. He does not want to fall into the sin of self-sufficiency and deny God as the provider. It is all for the honor of God's name. Proverbs 3:5–6 says, "Trust in the Lord with all your heart and do not lean on your own understanding. In all your ways acknowledge Him." It says in all ways, in every way, including money. The purpose of wealth is to honor God.

In my life experience, I have seen four ways people use money. The first is to satisfy themselves and use it how they want with little thought of God or others. The second is to build that extra cushion to feel safe and make sure you have all you need for the future. The trust is in the money and plan. And the third that I have heard in Christian circles is that money is bad. As a missionary and pastor's kid, I saw this a lot. Anyone working for God should suffer financially since money is something of the world and is evil. The trust is in the legalism of "suffering for God." The last is to acknowledge and honor God as the owner and provider. The trust is in God. Our ideas of money reveal who and what we trust.

Wealth is not about what we earn or receive from others. It is about what God gives us to steward. God owns my house, so I will use it how He, the owner, wants me to. God provided the job for me, so I will work unto Him. Stanley Tam tells the story in his book, *God Owns My Business*, how he legally put God as the owner of his business. It is a great illustration of acknowledging God as the owner and provider of wealth.

God is wealthy. He is the creator and owner of the earth. He wants us to manage His riches well. He has divided it among His stewards—men. God gives some more than He gives others. And because we live in a sinful world, some men take from others and use their wealth for evil. But for those who follow God, wealth is a tool to do His work. It can help people, support needs, run programs, and pay ministers.

Wealth is not only about our relationship with God but also about our relationship with others. It is stewardship with the idea of how that stewardship affects others. How does it affect your workers? How does it affect future generations? "Know well the condition of your flocks, and pay attention to your herds" (Proverbs 27:23). A good manager of wealth knows what is going on with his things. But he not only should be aware but act on it. Proverbs has called a wise person to be aware of others' needs and feelings through compassion and generosity.

Produce

God wants us to work and make money so we can own things and use them to promote His name and reputation. Proverbs 22:7 says, "The rich rules over the poor, and the borrower becomes the lender's slave." The idea is that the owner is better off. We don't want to be the borrower. We want to be the lender. We want to have enough money that we can lend it out.

In Luke 19, Jesus tells the parable of the talents. There was an owner who went away and gave each of his workers different amounts of denarii. When the owner returned, the workers who invested the denarii with the highest returns received a reward. Just as we are to produce life and health through our tongues and words, we are to produce with our money. God wants us to build something, not just spend it. "I passed by the field of the sluggard and by the vineyard of a man lacking sense, and behold, it was completely overgrown with thistles; its surface was covered with nettles, and its stone wall was broken down. When I saw, I reflected upon it; I looked, and received instructions. 'A little sleep, a little slumber, A little folding of the hands to rest,' Then your poverty will come as a robber and your want like an armed man" (Proverbs 24:30–34). God desires us to plant vineyards and build walls. In other words, there should be something to show for the wealth He has given us to manage. Our work should produce something, for example, start a business that solves a problem, grow a ministry that serves people, or create jobs for others. Generosity is not always giving things away but providing opportunities for wealth for others. Corrie Ten Boom hid Jews in Holland during WWII. Her family was caught and sent to a concentration camp. After the war, someone allowed Corrie to use their mansion. She used it to rehabilitate prisoners in concentration camps. When my family was in Spain on the mission field, we would go every summer for a week to a home on the beaches of Malaga. It was a vacation home with three apartments that were owned by a British couple who wanted missionaries to have a place to rest and refresh from their work. In *A Christmas Carol*, Charles Dickens writes of the ghost of Marley, Scrooge's business partner. Marley starts his "lessons" to Scrooge by describing what really is his business. "But you were always a good man of business, Jacob," faltered Scrooge. "Business!" cried the ghost, wringing its hands again. "Mankind was my business. The common welfare was my business; charity, mercy, forbearance, and benevolence were all my business. The dealings of my trade were but a drop of water in the comprehensive ocean of my business!"

The means of attaining wealth

Proverbs also speaks on the means of gaining wealth. There is a right and wrong way. One of my sons found a chain necklace in a parking lot. He was excited and insisted that he was going to sell this necklace on eBay for a lot of money. I kept telling him it was not real gold and no one would pay a lot of money for it. Getting rich quickly is not a norm. Proverbs 13:11 mentions that "Wealth obtained from nothing dwindles, But the one who gathers by labor increases it." Lasting wealth takes time. According to Ramsey Solutions "The National Study of Millionaires in 2018," they studied 10,000 millionaires, and out of those, 79 percent received no inheritance. They had to work for their money. Eight out of ten invested in their company's 401(k). The top five careers for millionaires were engineers, CPAs, teachers, management positions, and attorneys. Only 31 percent made more than $100,000 per year. In the study, Dave Ramsey says, "Human nature is that we want to hit the easy button. We want to know the shortest possible path to wealth. I want to show you the shortest, fastest, correct route that gets you to a million-dollar net worth. Just know, it's actually a slow, steady process—like 'The Tortoise and the Hare' fable."[2] Proverbs speaks of other wrong means to attain wealth, including cheating, oppressing the poor, and rewarding the rich.

Laziness

Within the topic of wealth and work, Proverbs mentions laziness as one of the main problems.

---

[2] Dave Ramsey, "The National Study of Millionaires—The American Dream Is Alive and Available," Ramsey Solutions (2018), https://www.ramseysolutions.com/retirement/the-national-study-of-millionaires-research.

The wings of wealth

Proverbs 23:4–6 says, "Do not weary yourself to gain wealth. Cease from your consideration of it. When you set your eyes on it, it is gone. For wealth certainly makes itself wings Like an eagle that flies toward the heavens." There has to be a balance between working hard and resting since wealth does not last forever. Solomon brings in a little of his Ecclesiastical ideas here. Enjoy what you have worked for.

Concluding prayer

Dear Lord,

You own it all. Help me to acknowledge You and honor You with the wealth You give me. Help me to manage it well. Help me to share and help others with it. Help me to produce something with it. Give me wisdom to pass these truths on to my children. In Jesus's name, amen.

Verse to pray: Ecclesiastes 9:10

Practical Proverbs for the family

Below are some Bible stories to discuss with younger children to help them become acquainted with wealth.

The naive and youth
- Read stories of people who worked hard and used what they had for God and others:

    ○ Abraham shares with Lot (Genesis 13).
    ○ God blesses Jacob (Genesis 30).
    ○ Joseph manages Egypt's resources during the famine (Genesis 47).

- David pays for land on which he sacrifices (2 Samuel 24).

The wise
- Read the following verses about the lazy one. What are some images given? What do you think about God's desire for us to produce versus being lazy?

Proverbs 12:11, 27   Proverbs 19:15, 24
Proverbs 14:23   Proverbs 20:4, 13
Proverbs 16:26   Proverbs 21:17, 25
Proverbs 18:9   Proverbs 24:33–34

Parent reflection and application

- *Discuss your ideas about wealth.* Define what makes wealth good and bad. What is the purpose of wealth? Use Scripture to back up your answer.
- What will you produce with your wealth? Ministry, business, a home where people can stay, a place for Bible study?
- What are your children good at? Could they start a business, a garden, or an instruction video? Could they produce something?

CHAPTER 17

A Warrior Woman—
Do Not Give Your Strength Away

An excellent wife, who can find?

—Proverbs 31:10

Principle: The Proverbs 31 woman is not a list that women must adhere to but is, rather, the permission and celebration of God's intent for a woman to be a powerful warrior for her family.

The first thing I will say about Proverbs 31 is that it was not written by Solomon. Aren't you glad, women, that the chapter on the wife was not written by the man who had six hundred of them? It was written by a man, King Lemuel, but they are the words of his mother. These are the words of a mother to her son. It is noteworthy to see that this chapter is an acrostic poem. That means it is written in alphabetical order, each line starting with a letter of the Hebrew alphabet. Acrostic poems were used as a tool to help memorize. This chapter was something that King Lemuel's mom wanted her son to remember. God has used Solomon's writing to his son to teach us about wisdom and His way of life. In this last chapter, he uses a woman to illustrate all the concepts he has been teaching. Think of a children's book and the beautiful illustrations in them. This chapter is the beautifully colored-in illustration of Proverbs. When your little ones say, "Let me see the picture," the woman is the picture of this book.

The only commands in this chapter are directed at King Lemuel, "Do not give your strength to that which destroys" and "Open your mouth for the weak." King Lemuel's mother starts by telling him two things that will ruin him: giving away his strength to the wrong woman and giving way to that which would destroy him—drunkenness. Then she reminds him of his responsibility to those he rules over.

The king is not to give away his strength to the wrong woman. The word for "strength" here means efficiency, wealth, or army. He should not share his ability, moral worth, wealth, or power with a woman who will destroy these. She is not saying he should not share his life with a woman. In verse 10, she encourages him to find a wife, but he is to be on the lookout for a certain type of woman—one that is strong in contrast to one who will take his strength away. This word for a strong woman is the same word for strength that is not to be given away. In essence, she is saying, "Do not give your *chayil* (strength) away. Find a woman of *chayil* (strength)." He is to find a wife of strength, power, moral worth, and wealth. She is a warrior!

The wife should have the strength to fight for the things that matter in life. She is to be a warrior in the marriage relationship and a warrior for her family. She is to fight for and build up those in her sphere of influence. She stewards these things and fights for them as a warrior would. She is not to suck the energy or the resources of her husband and leave him with nothing. She is to stand next to him in battle and lift him up as he would her. Please do not misunderstand. I am not saying that wives can never cry, be weak, or in need. This warrior woman is strong in character and morals. She should be a partner, producer, and warrior for the things that concern her family and community. This woman makes the world she lives in.

I have heard many women look at this chapter as a to-do list to be the perfect godly woman, but remember, these are not commands but a picture. I would like to focus on women in the Bible who exemplified the characteristics shared in this chapter.

Her character

In Proverbs 31, a woman has strength, dignity, confidence, and trustworthiness. The wife King Lemuel should find has the same character qualities as a wise person. Above all, she fears the Lord. It is interesting that Proverbs 1 starts with the fear of the Lord. It is the beginning of knowledge and wisdom, the foundation for all. And now Proverbs is ending with this woman who fears the Lord. "Charm is deceitful and beauty is vain, but a woman who fears the Lord, she shall be praised" (Proverbs 31:30). All other things will fade away—beauty and charm—but her fear of the Lord is what will last. This woman knows God's place and hers. She trusts in Him, does not fear, and even laughs at the future. Yet she prepares and is ready for what may come her way. She knows that trust is not an excuse to be lazy. Maybe she was able to do so much because she did not waste her time worrying and fearing. She trusted God, putting Him in His place. And she fulfilled her responsibilities, knowing her place.

She reminds me of Hannah. In 1 Samuel 1, Hannah was distraught because she did not have children. She went to the temple to pray, fast, and plead with the Lord. Scripture says that she was greatly distressed and wept bitterly. Eli, the priest, saw her praying and thought that she was drunk because her lips were moving, but no sound was coming out. She had probably been weeping so much she could not even speak. Hannah responded that she was "oppressed in spirit…and poured out her soul to the Lord." After Hannah prayed and spoke with Eli, the Bible says she "went her way and ate, and her face was no longer sad." Her entire countenance changed. She was distressed, oppressed, and appeared drunk to bystanders. What happened? What changed? She did not get her request answered that quickly. She laid her request before God and put it in His hands. She trusted and let go. She let go of the worry and all the physical manifestations it produced in her. Her physical demeanor changed when she put her trust in her God. She did not stay in her sorrow. She conquered it with the strength of trust in the Lord. Psalm 46:10 says, "Cease striving and know that I am God." The idea is to relax and let go and know who is in charge. This is what a woman who fears the Lord does.

Because the fear of the Lord is crucial, I will give another example of a woman who fears God. Esther was a young Jewish girl who faced her fears at tremendous cost. She put her self-interest and protection aside as she put the needs of her countrymen first. A strong woman cares for others. Esther's famous words in Esther 4:16: "Go, assemble all the Jews who are found in Susa, and fast for me; do not eat or drink for three days, night or day. I and my maidens also will fast in the same way. And thus I will go in to the king, which is not according to the law; and if I perish, I perish." Mordecai had given Esther the challenge that God had placed her there to save the Jews. She made a decision and took charge of the situation. Mordecai never told her the details of what to do; he only challenged her to do something. Esther came up with the plan and demonstrated that she knew God's place in the situation by asking for prayer and fasting first. She displayed the plans and the preparations a warrior would make in a battle.

Her relationships

In her relationship with her husband, she is trustworthy. She builds him up and does him good. Her reputation precedes her. Men talk about her at the gates. He, in turn, blesses her and praises her. Her children call her "happy."

Abigail demonstrated this wisdom in her relationship with her husband. In 1 Samuel 25, Nabal, Abigail's husband, is approached by David's men. He is a wealthy man who owned many sheep. While David was in the wilderness, he had come across his shepherds and had cared for them. David's men approached Nabal to ask if he would provide hospitality for them so they could celebrate one of the feasts. Nabal, being a harsh and evil man according to the Bible, denied their request and insulted David. So David planned to repay Nabal accordingly. He got his army ready to attack and kill Nabal. Abigail heard what happened and went to David with food loaded on donkeys: "When Abigail saw David, she hurried and dismounted from her donkey and fell on her face before David and bowed herself to the ground. She fell at his feet and said, 'On me alone, my Lord, be the blame. And please let your maidservant speak to you, and listen to the words of your maidservant. Please forgive the transgression of your maidservant; for the Lord will certainly make for my lord an enduring house, because my lord is fighting battles of the Lord, and evil will not be found in you all your days'" (1 Samuel 25:23–28). Abigail stopped David from avenging himself, apologized for something she did not do, and brought David the food he had requested. In doing so, she saved her husband's life, although God killed him the next day! In addition, she saved David's reputation as a man who did not do evil. Her plea refocused David on his mission to fight the Lord's battles, not his own. She did good to Nabal, her husband, and to David, who later became her husband. She avoided the likely bloodshed of her servants and David's men. She used her wisdom of relationships to calm man's anger. Abigail was a woman who did not take strength from others. She was a woman of strength.

Her responsibility

We see that the woman King Lemuel's mother describes works in the home and outside. She serves her family well and manages the home well. She creates things with her own hands, including food and clothing. But she also works with the community in the business realm and buys and sells things. She works hard and gets up early. She is prepared for the seasons and plans ahead.

When I think of Ruth, I think of the sweetest, kindest person you would ever meet. She seems like that person with an incredibly likable personality. One thing that I admire about her is her willingness to provide for herself and for Naomi in the most dire and difficult of circumstances. After losing her husband and sons, Naomi pities herself. In Ruth 1:20–21, Naomi says to the women in Bethlehem, "Do not call me Naomi; call me Mara, for the Almighty has dealt very bitterly with me. I went out full, but the Lord has brought me back empty. Why do you call me Naomi, since the Lord has witnessed against me and the Almighty has afflicted me?" Naomi lost a lot, but here she says she came home empty. She had a daughter-in-law who came back with her, who made an incredible promise to go with her, lodge with her, die with her, make her people hers, and take her God (Ruth 1:16–17). Ruth had also lost a husband and yet does not have this attitude of self-pity. She reasonably could be depressed, down, discouraged, and fearful. She was a widow with no means of provision, no man to comfort her or provide for her, and a mother-in-law who was not doing much to help. Ruth picked herself up and took the initiative to go to Boaz's field to glean among the harvesters and get them some food (Ruth 2:2). If left up to Naomi, they would have starved to death in self-pity. This attitude and initiative were recognized by Boaz, who found it attractive. Boaz inquired about this woman he had noticed. He went through the process to redeem and wed her. God provided a blessing through Ruth's willingness and wise attitude to fight. Do you see the quality King Lemuel's mother is talking about—a woman who fights for her family, a woman who is not a victim? Do you see the Proverbs valiant warrior in Ruth?

After looking at these examples, can you see the principles in Proverbs 31? A warrior woman works for God, whether it is making clothes, answering phones, or changing diapers. She is empowered by God because she fears Him. She knows who God is, so she can trust Him. Her community, the men of the city, her family, and her children all respect and honor her. They speak well of her because they see her work, her view of God, and her influence. This is a life picture of wisdom. It is not a daily picture of her; it is a life picture.

Do we work through this list and try to become this woman? No! We look at the beginning of Proverbs and the end. "The fear of the Lord is the beginning of knowledge" (Proverbs 1: 7). "A woman who fears the Lord, she shall be praised" (Proverbs 31:30b). We start with fearing God. Then we give strength instead of taking it.

Concluding prayer

> Dear Lord,
>
> Please help me to be a woman of strength for my family and community. Help me to give strength and not take it. I am weak on my own

and need You. Therefore, please help me to fear You in all I do, to put You first, trust You, rely on You, and above all, honor You. In Jesus's name, amen.

Verse to pray: Pick one from Proverbs 31 that the Lord lays on your heart.

Practical Proverbs for the family

Because this section is for the wise, older kids, I have not included practical things for younger children. The focus for them is the earlier part in Proverbs. But this does not mean you cannot read it or find something you can use.

The wise
- Read through chapter 31. Write down the character qualities of the woman—how she dealt with relationships and responsibilities. Compare these to the chart on wisdom in chapter 10. Use these to talk to your children about what a wise woman looks like, whether you have boys or girls.

Wise Character	Wise Relationships	Wise Responsibility

Parent reflection and application

- Identify: What season of life are you in? What are your circles of influence (students, children, friends, elderly family)? What are your responsibilities?

- How can you give strength to the people in your circle? How can you show strength in your responsibilities?
- If you are a man, what commands were given to men in this chapter? How can you follow them?

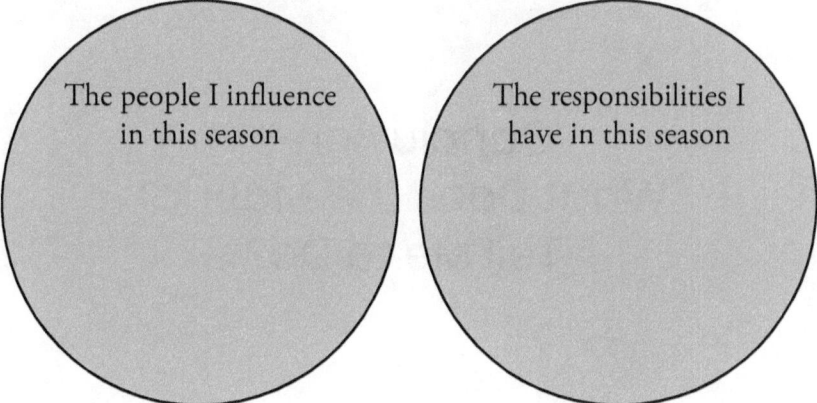

CHAPTER 18

Conclusion— What Does the Manual Tell Me to Do?

> Train up a child in the way he should go, even when he is old he will not depart from it.
>
> —Proverbs 22:6

    This is the famous claim to raising our kids in God's way. I struggled with this verse because I have seen people who have raised their children in a godly way, yet their children have not followed God. If we believe that we have free will and our children have free will, then this verse cannot be a promise that if we do it well it will all turn our right. So, is it a fake promise? What does it mean?

    Some have claimed that it means training each child in their individual way, as in helping them figure out their bent (what they are good at) and disciplining them in an individual way that is effective for their personality. I don't see that in the verse, and I don't see it elsewhere in Proverbs. The word "train" does not imply individuality. Actually, the fact that it says "the" way and not "a" way implies that it is a definite way for everyone. There is no claim to do things differently for each child. The whole idea of a proverb is that it is true throughout the ages and for all people. Proverb means "a short, pithy saying in frequent and widespread use that expresses a basic truth or practical precept." So again, what does it mean?

The word for "train" here is not the typical word used for training in Proverbs. Normally, the word for *instruct* or *train* is *yasar*. This word in Proverbs 22:6 is not used anywhere else in Proverbs. It is the word *chanak*. It is used elsewhere in Scripture and mostly translated as "dedicate," referring to dedicating a home or the temple. It comes from a word that means to "rub the palate of a newborn." It was a custom in the Middle East when a baby was born to rub its palate with dates, oil, or honey to stimulate the baby's sucking reflex. Therefore, the verse is saying to train up a child or dedicate them to the way they should go. The way is what Proverbs has been talking about—the way of wisdom—God's way.

Proverbs is full of verses that speak about the way or path we should go in. In fact, fifty-five verses mention paths or ways. This meaning makes sense in the light of the whole book. The whole book is about wisdom, choosing God's way over man's.

But how do we train? Go back to the meaning of the word *chanak*. We are to give them a taste of the sweetness of God's ways from the beginning. Incline them to get their nourishment from God by giving them a taste for its sweetness. The word "dedicate" is defined as devoting time, effort, or oneself to a task or purpose. We are devoting time, effort, and ourselves for the purpose of having our kids walk in God's ways. We are guiding their walk, holding their hand, and having them follow the road. As they grow, we walk to the side and talk with them about what we see on life's path, explaining how it aligns with God's ways and what benefits or consequences there are. Then as they mature, we step back and walk behind them, sometimes giving a warning, answering a question, helping to steer them when they get to a fork in the road. We are always a companion but by different means and measures.

So does this verse guarantee certain results? It does in a proverbial way. Proverbial truths are true in most cases. It is a general truth of cause and effect that if you brush your teeth twice a day and floss, you won't get cavities, but there are times it does not work out as the norm. Please don't misunderstand. I am not saying that the Bible and truth are relative. The Bible is absolute truth. But within the Bible are literary language tools. A proverb is one of those tools. The essence of proverbs is that they are comparisons of cause and effect. They happen most of the time.

Think of it this way: if you give your child a taste of love, truth, and God, they will likely follow it. If you give your child a taste of manipulation, guilt, and condemnation, they will likely follow it. If you show your child anger, outbursts, yelling, and disapproval, that is what they will likely follow and be like in their relationships.

The way a child is brought up—habits, teachings, and examples—are what they will most likely follow. In summary, devote your energy to inclining your child to God's way. Give them the best taste you can for God's way by example and much talk and instruction. Then when he is old, having tasted and seen how good it is, he is very likely to continue in it (Proverbs 22:6).

My conclusions from Proverbs are many, but I have several steps or main points that a parent can follow. Proverbs is about God's way versus man's way. There are two ways to go in life. Which one will you choose? Which one will you teach and train your children in?

Step 1: *End goal first*. You must know the end goal. Remember Proverbs 1, where Solomon lists all the dos? What is your end goal with your kids? What do you want them to leave with?

Step 2: *Foundation*. Second, you must lay a foundation for God's way. Teach your children the four foundational things: fearing the Lord, listening, being aware, and using wisdom.

Step 3: *Two ways*. Compare the two ways to go in life: God's way and man's, the wise and the foolish. Use Proverbs's examples and sayings, especially chapters 10–15.

Step 4: *Character*. Talk about character attributes such as self-control, integrity, productivity, and so on, and develop habits in them.

Step 5: *Charge them with stewardship.* Charge your children with responsibility, wealth, work, and relationships. Teach them that it all is stewardship.

Step 6: *Appeal and inspire.* Appeal to the whole person—the heart and inner man, including mind, will, and emotions. They are all to be sanctified by the Holy Spirit. We want to inspire a true change of heart that only God can do. We ultimately want to inspire obedience to God by knowing Him (chapter 16). Parents are God's first instrument to prime the heart, inspire, and lead by example. Motivate through God's promise of eternal and lasting rewards (chapter 4).

Step 7: *Follow the process.* Finally, follow the process of building the foundation and growing independence. Start by instructing and laying the foundation of facts and knowledge in the early stages. Then build on that by conversing about character and comparing God's way and man's. Then step back and become the adviser. Trust your efforts and God's ability by letting go of your child. Let them practice in the safety of your home before they have to do it completely on their own. Remember, the fear of the Lord is the key.

ABOUT THE AUTHOR

Kristin Overman is married to her best friend, Tim. Together, they have six children, five boys and a girl. Kristin and Tim homeschool their children and started the nonprofit Abundant Homes to serve homeschool families. They are transplants to Raleigh, North Carolina after having lived in Albuquerque, New Mexico for over 30 years. They enjoy spending time outside in their gardens, playing in the river or in the mountains, hiking, and camping. Kristin loves to read, write, and learn, especially about the Bible. She enjoys serving others by teaching and speaking.

www.ingramcontent.com/pod-product-compliance
Lightning Source LLC
LaVergne TN
LVHW091550060526
838200LV00036B/778